A Modern Girl's Guide
to Getting Organised

Sarah Ivens is the Editor-in-Chief of *OK!* magazine in America. She has written for *Tatler*, *GQ*, *Cosmopolitan*, *Marie Claire*, *Men's Health*, *InStyle*, the *Daily Mail* and the *Mirror*. She is a born and bred Londoner who now lives in New York City.

Sarah's first five books, *A Modern Girl's Guide to Getting Hitched*, *A Modern Girl's Guide to Networking*, *A Modern Girl's Guide to Dynamic Dating*, *A Modern Girl's Guide to Etiquette* and *The Bride's Guide to Unique Weddings* are also published by Piatkus.

A Modern Girl's Guide to Getting Organised

How to save time and stress ... and avoid sleepless nights

SARAH IVENS

PIATKUS

PIATKUS

First published in Great Britain in 2007 by Piatkus Books

Copyright © Sarah Ivens

A CIP catalogue record for this book
is available from the British Library

ISBN 978-0-7499-2917-9

Edited by Jan Cutler
Illustrations by Megan Hess
Text designed and set by Paul Saunders

Printed and bound in Great Britain by
Clays Ltd, St Ives plc

Piatkus Books
An imprint of
Little, Brown Book Group
100 Victoria Embankment
London EC4Y ODY

An Hachette Livre UK Company

www.piatkus.co.uk

Dedication

For my favourite super-efficient señoritas:
Helen Ivens and Claire Steele.

Contents

Acknowledgements

Thanks to my organised editor, Alice Davis, and the wonderfully efficient team at Piatkus for helping me with my sixth book for them ... wow, we must be organised! Cheers, as always, to Megan Hess for her lovely illustrations.

A big shout to my wonderfully time-sensitive, non-stressed pals across the pond for their invaluable input: Mel, Jo, Ros, May, Shirley, Anna and Nikky, and my charmingly together friends Stateside: Katie, Juliet, Jaqui, Jen, Holly, Shania and Roberta.

And, as always, to my lovely family x.

Introduction

A FULLY FUNCTIONING modern girl needs to learn little tricks to save time and reduce stress when she's planning anything, from a meeting or a holiday to a night out with the girls.

If you've ever felt anxious because of a few undone chores, *A Modern Girl's Guide to Getting Organised* is for you. If you've ever thrown a wobbly because you couldn't find anything to eat in your fridge, read this book extra-quick. If a messy knicker drawer sends you into a weeping mass of Ferrero Rocher-munching depression, help is at hand!

As more and more demands are placed at the feet of the modern girl (we must climb the career ladder, look gorgeous, conduct a healthy relationship, be a social butterfly and think about when is the right time to have children), a set of rules and guidelines are needed to navigate success – and a sense of peace – without going stark raving mad.

I've certainly been known to burst into tears when things haven't gone my way, be it a flat tyre or a misplaced set of keys. Feeling out of control is scary, even when the things we've lost control over are small things like tyres and keys.

Modern girls fear that these little things will lead to bigger things, and soon we'll be running through the streets with bush-backwards hair, mismatched stilettos and a look of menace, screaming, 'I can keep it together, honest, guv! I can do it all, I can have it all!'

My poor best friend had to witness an 'unreasonable' outburst of moaning and hysteria recently because I lost my trainers. You'd have thought the cat had been run over for the amount of histrionics coming from the downstairs closet – I was inconsolable! And, of course, my overreaction led into insecurity on other things: was I good enough at my job, why did I always burn lasagne, was I where I should be at my age? Itchy, raw emotions of unworthiness swirled around me in darkness. Oh yes, Fun Saturday (as it's now referred to in our house) shows how being thoughtless and unprepared about the smallest things can build up into other areas of your life. What have I learned from that experience? Always keep my shoes in one place, and go to the gym in the morning before I get emotional and tired at night. Oh yes, and life is more fun when you're organised! I am not a naturally organised person, but as more and more responsibilities have been thrown on my shoulders, I've had to learn to improve.

Thankfully, my mother was born with a feather duster in one hand and her diary in the other … and her precise nature has become something worth mimicking as I've got a little older. She is the Queen of Lists and punctuality, she never forgets a birthday or bites off more than she can chew, and I admire that immensely. She's made me appreciate how a lovely, calm home is important – but an ordered mind is a necessity.

Now I can happily (well, if not happily then efficiently) get up and go to the gym, get to work on time and have a day of meetings, problem solving and forward planning, enjoying a lunch with friends at half-time. I can then head home to a neat apartment and be able to truly enjoy a bubble bath and an issue of *OK!* with an ethereal sense of calm – while the laundry is spinning away in the washer and a home-cooked supper is in the oven.

Packed full of advice, time-saving ideas and stress-reducing plans – as well as personal stories from real-life super-organised women – this book will help you in all areas of your life, from your work to your wardrobe, from your home to your holidays.

Being organised is not about being a nerdy geek – it's about not sweating the small stuff so that you can get on with living life to the max. It's about never having those sweaty panic attacks at 6.00 a.m. ever again ... and that's got to be good, correct?

Happy organising, dudellas!

Chapter One

Everyday skills for an easy life

AH, THE BLISS OF A well-organised diary or a neatly ticked-off 'to-do' list! Life doesn't get much better than that, you know. Being organised saves time, stress, mishaps and mayhem. Bring a little organisation into your life!

The beauty of to-do lists

I've always been a list fanatic. Since I was a child, I'd enjoy the process of getting into school early and making an ordered list of what I needed to achieve that day. From planning a birthday party (well, giving my ideas to my mother) to remembering to take my gym kit home, there was something comforting about having your day, your week and your gruesome chores all set out clearly. Order meant an end to chaos – and getting told off by the parents if I forgot to give them a letter from my teacher.

How to make the perfect list:

1. Number each item carefully so that it is very easy to read – and watch the handwriting (there's no point writing if it's just an illegible scrawl).

2. Keep it somewhere obvious and close to hand, so that you can add and subtract things when necessary. In your handbag is a good idea, or I like to write mine on a Post-it note or sticky pad and attach it to my computer screen (which is, sadly, the thing I look at most during the average working day).

3. If you have a tendency for procrastination, use your list as an alarm clock: next to each task, put an allotted time. Give yourself a realistic goal for item numbers 1–5, then the rest of the day to complete the list.

4. Promise yourself a reward when you're halfway done – this will keep you motivated. I don't suggest a Hermes scarf, just a five-minute walk around the block or a cappuccino from the coffee machine.

5. Don't keep a to-do list by your bed if it'll bring you out in night sweats – you need some time to relax, for Pete's sake. But do keep a notepad and pen on your bedside cabinet if you are prone to last-minute thoughts or early-morning moments of inspiration.

6. Give yourself a day off from to-do lists – Sunday being the obvious choice. Everyone needs to have some time to throw caution to the wind and risk a lie-in.

7. If it makes you feel better and psyches you up to complete the list, feel free to sort of 'cheat' and add tasks you've already half-done, or feel worthy about completing earlier on in the day. It's your list – who cares?

8. If you're feeling swamped, divide your tasks into two lists: things you must do today, and things for some time this week.

9. Don't beat yourself up if you haven't got through everything you wanted to, just focus on how to save time to get through it more efficiently the next time (tips on this to come).

10. Relish throwing your list away when it's all completed. Well done!

NB In all areas of life, not just when you're making a handy list, it's a good idea to get the bad and boring jobs done first – then you'll feel worthy and wonderful and more able to take on the less strenuous deeds. Believe me, after doing three ugly jobs, chore four (calling your granny to see how she is) will seem like bliss.

Ticking off chores

When they're done, they're done – my personal preference is for drawing a line through them with a luminous marker, that way my good work is really highlighted. Other people like to put a tick next to the number, or to tear off that piece of paper. Whatever you do, don't cheat and tick things off before you've really done them – that defeats the whole purpose and will deflate any good feelings you have about being so well organised. Sometimes, it's good to keep your to-do lists in a notebook, which you can refer to from week to week, or season to season – especially if you are noting useful phone numbers or websites that you will need again. It can also remind you when you need to start looking for particular things or buy things, and so on.

HOLLY, 32

❝I'm not the most organised person. That's no secret. But I love making lists. I have a standard grocery list. On Fridays I make a list of what I want to do for the weekend. I have your run-of-the-mill to-do list. I keep a list of gifts that friends and family might like for Christmas and birthdays. In college I wrote a list of the people I wanted to go out with – luckily, I only checked off three of the 57! I have a list of clothing I need to buy. Then there's a list of things that will make my messy apartment more liveable. And I couldn't forget the "things that make me happy" list. But what's my favourite one? The most wanted food list: it covers all of the treats that put a smile on my face. Granted, I rarely indulge, as I am trying to lose weight and my choices don't shun trans-fats. I guess that means that fighting the battle of the bulge will be my new year's resolution for the tenth consecutive year!

Other useful lists

The to-do list is the classic organised-person's piece of paper, but lists can be used for everything. One very 'together' friend keeps a list in the big food cupboard in her kitchen (and a similar one on top of the freezer) and makes a note of the date when things were put in there and the date they need to be eaten by (more on food in Chapter 3).

Another very glamorous friend keeps a clothes list – stating her different outfits and which accessories she wore with them that looked great. This saves time if you're in a hurry and need to get out of the door looking fab.

A useful list that I have started making is on the last day of my holiday. Grabbing a bit of the hotel stationery, I'll quickly note down how many pairs of shoes I wore, how many jumpers I really needed, and if I lugged too many toiletries across the ocean. You do forget, and this list helps me pack the next time. People always remark on what a neat and concise packer I am, and I'm sure it's because my lists remind me what will be pointless in my luggage.

Memories are made of this

The organised-girl's biggest must-have is a good memory – without it she's lost. Literally. Even if you weren't born with the ability to recite a phone book, there are a few things a healthy brain needs to keep you on track:

◆ **Sleep well.** Your brain strengthens while you're sleeping. Get your eight hours, or else. No amount of caffeine or chocolate will make you an Einstein in meetings if you're burning the candle at both ends.

◆ **Try not to get too stressed.** When you're freaking out, the brain releases a hormone called cortisol. This hormone can slowly damage the part of the brain that is in charge of short-term memory. Take more time out, more long soaks in the tub and less notice of your boss or your nagging mother (more on this later).

◆ **Get physical.** You wanna get physical if you wanna get memory-smart. When you exercise, feel-good hormones flood your body, giving you the impetus to get moving in all aspects of your life. Plus, exercising supplies oxygen and nutrients to your brain.

◆ **Play sudoku.** Keeping your memory in tip-top form can be helped by setting yourself little mental agility tests. So, be like a granny: get out that chessboard, fill in that crossword, and enter your local pub's quiz – it's all good for long-term memory!

Memory aids

You don't have to rely on mental agility alone when it comes to being organised; there are a few tricks to help you remember special occasions – and where you've put the cat:

◆ Invest in a birthday book. These are fabulously useful and fun. You can get all kinds of birthday books; some have a star-sign snippet for each month, plus a little prediction for each actual day – you can send this message with a birthday email on a friend's special day! You can get these from any good stationers or department store.

◆ Your brain will forget little bits of info. It's not built to store random data, so you have to make a conscious effort to imprint important things into your consciousness. Whenever you have to learn a new bank pin or phone number, write down the number five times and look at it – seriously, stare at it like a mad woman for a good 30 seconds. It's also a good idea to keep such important numbers written down in a top-secret place just in case the mind does fail you!

◆ As soon as a friend gives you his or her new email address or moving-home card, carefully copy the details into your filing system – be it a file on your computer or an old-fashioned address book. Otherwise, you will lose the info and end up having to ask them again. Save yourself the hassle and do it right the first time.

◆ Visualise things. When you're learning someone's name or details about their life, try to build a little story or visual reference to match it and make it easier to take hold in your head. The first time you meet someone, really focus on their face (without appearing creepy) and repeat their name a few times in conversation in the first few minutes.

◆ Make life simpler by building little routines. This could be a rule as simple as always putting your door keys in the same place when you walk in at night, to checking your diary every Monday morning for important meetings that require a dry-cleaned suit, dates that require hair-free legs or friends who require birthday cards. Getting into a system really helps the most forgetful Fiona!

◆ Who hasn't had a panic halfway to the bus stop that she's left her hair straighteners on and the house is about to burn down? I think we all have! The problem is that simple tasks like locking the front door or unplugging the iron uses procedural memory and is more automatic than thought about. If you're really starting to worry about whether you have or haven't done what you are supposed to do, start stating the case out loud as you're doing it: 'The kettle is off', 'My iPod is in my handbag', and so on.

JEN, 31

❝Saying that you're bad about remembering things like birthdays apparently isn't as good an excuse as it once was. The other day a friend told me her birthday had passed about four days earlier, when I was out of town. I'm not sure she had ever even told me when her birthday was, but she was clearly annoyed that I hadn't acknowledged it. When I asked her why she had never mentioned it and how I was supposed to know, she said, "Well, it was on myspace!" The lesson: sign up for myspace or facebook birthday alerts and check often.❞

Time management

There really aren't enough hours in the day! As your commitments increase, so does your anxiety about being able to squeeze them all in. But you must take a stand and rule time, before time rules you.

How to prioritise

◆ **Get ugly jobs done first.** Literally power through them without stopping. If you leave it too long, you'll talk yourself out of them and leave them for another day.

◆ **Put up reminders in your office,** on the fridge or on the front door, about the day's goals.

◆ **Stop regretting time wasted or your failures.** It's even more of a waste of time. Learn from your mistakes and move on.

◆ **Concentrate on one thing at a time.**

◆ **Look ahead in your monthly calendar** and predict what might happen – a holiday, a friend staying, a busy time in the office, and so on – and work these into your schedule to make sure you leave yourself enough time.

◆ **Don't dilly-dally.** Have confidence in your first decision.

◆ **If you have a big project, start with the hardest part first.** You'll make the easier parts even easier, or totally redundant.

◆ **Stop activities that have no benefit to you,** or that you can sense will be unproductive. Get out while the going's good.

- ◆ **Spend more time on areas of your life that will have long-term benefits** (such as friendships and relationships with your family).

- ◆ **Ask for help** when you need it – don't be ashamed.

- ◆ **Think on paper.** Note down your agenda or your plan, it's easier to rethink and revise when it's out clearly in front of you.

- ◆ **Push yourself.** The mind and the body can actually squeeze a lot more into a day than we may give it credit for.

Procrastination problems

If you catch yourself procrastinating, think, 'What am I avoiding?' If you can't come up with a logical, realistic answer, you could just be exhausted – so give yourself a break. We all have days when we can't get motivated, and sometimes it's best to admit defeat and completely remove ourselves from the task, to return fresh and reinvigorated.

If, however, it's clear you are avoiding something, do one of two things. Number one: follow a rule above, grab the bull by the horns and just do it – get the ugly jobs done first. Then give yourself a reward: a glass of wine or a read through a new magazine. Number two: if this project is making you miserable, work to get yourself out of this situation. Find something to enjoy in whatever you do, and don't continue in a grey world of unhappiness once you've acknowledged what the problem is.

How to do things quickly

◆ **Don't lose focus.** When you're doing a job, you'll save time if you turn off the TV; also don't answer the phone and don't talk to your colleagues while you're doing it.

◆ **If it helps to number tasks** and clearly define what needs to be done for each first, take a minute to do that.

◆ **Try not to make life any harder than it is.** Some things need to be done perfectly; other things (cleaning your flat, for example) just need to be done well.

◆ **Playing upbeat music loudly** can motivate some people to move faster – and to forget they're doing a troublesome job in the first place.

◆ **Don't sit down.** If you can, keep physically moving and you won't lose momentum.

Being on time

There's nothing worse than being late – for an organised person, anyway. You'll have nervous sweats, break into a run that ruins your high heels and you'll bite your nails to the quick, nervous that even a five-minute delay will seem careless to the person who is waiting for you.

The easiest thing to do is to set your clock a few minutes fast – you will forget you've done this, and having a few extra seconds as a cushion is invaluable. Also, be realistic, if you have meeting at 5.00 p.m., you are not going to get across town for dinner by 6.00 p.m., so make it 7.00 p.m.! And don't keep changing plans. Pick a decent time and stick to it – other people have busy lives to organise, too, you know! Always have money and a mobile phone on you, plus a travel card if one would be useful where you live – it's amazing how queuing at a cashpoint or train station can make a punctual person ten minutes late.

Keep everyone's numbers – even the numbers of bars and restaurants you visit regularly – in your phone, and update them when necessary. If you are late, inform the person you're meeting as soon as possible – or if you can't reach them, call ahead to the place you are meeting and leave a message. The basic rule to remember is: you are super-woman (of course!) but you can't be in three places at the same time, so be sensible when planning your diary and don't overfill your days. The stress of rushing is hideous!

JACKIE, 35

❝ I consider being late the height of rudeness! You're essentially saying that someone else's time is not as valuable as yours. Leave an extra ten minutes to get yourself to any destination. If, for some reason, you just can't help being late (traffic, etc.) give your friend a call right away! ❞

Dear diary...

Keep a diary – I couldn't live without mine. Colour code activities, and highlight the most important things in fluorescent pen. Keep your diary in the place you can access it most easily, be that your handbag or your desk at work. Get a diary that has public holidays listed in it, and one that's big enough to write a few separate things for each day – it's amazing how quickly it gets filled up with birthdays and dinner parties, plus work events. As soon as a date is set, put it in – neatly, so that you can read it a week, maybe a month, later. Illegible scrawl is pointless. If a date gets cancelled, cross it out immediately. I've shown up to cancelled events before and it's very annoying – a total waste of time (and money if you have to pay to get there).

Getting life under control

Of course, the whole point of being organised is to allow you to get your things under control, to stop the night sweats and blind panic when you realise you've forgotten your dad's birthday. That's why I believe having a well-organised to-do list and an easy-to-read diary is such a joy, and a must-have for the modern girl. They get all the bad stuff and chores of life out of the way so that when you do have the time and energy to chill out or go mad, you can do so without any nagging doubts of work unfinished. Get organised, and you don't have to take life so seriously.

Don't sweat the small stuff

◆ Get the important things sorted and let the smaller things take care of themselves. Be angry with yourself if you forget your keys, but don't waste time being annoyed if you forgot a magazine – buy another one on the way to work!

◆ The most important things in life (you realise as you get older) are family, friends and your good health – prioritise these over all else.

◆ If your work and its demands on you are too much, and you can feel all the other areas of your life being pulled out of sync, re-evaluate what you want and what you need. Don't lose friendships or partners because you gave too much time and energy to a boss who will never truly appreciate you anyway.

◆ You can't be good at everything – nobody is perfect. Allow yourself to foul up sometimes without guilt and regret kicking in.

◆ If you're feeling run-down or depressed, say, 'mañana, mañana' – nearly everything can wait until morning!

TEN SIMPLE TIPS FOR AVOIDING STRESS

1. **Exercise.** This sounds as if it could be stressful in itself, but it actually releases feel-good chemicals that make you relax and sleep better.

2. **Breathe deeply.** If it's all getting too much, stop what you are doing for a few minutes. Breathe in slowly for five seconds, hold for five, and then release slowly over five seconds. Repeat this ten times and you'll feel yourself relaxing.

3. **Get a pet.** Studies show that stroking and playing with a pet, a cat, dog, rabbit or gerbil (and even looking at gold-fish in a tank) have a soothing influence on the mind and body.

4. **Be positive.** Think the best, not the worst. Reinstall your faith with good affirmations such as, 'I am capable' or, 'We will make it through this difficult time.'

5. **Make a note of when you feel most stressed.** Is a pattern emerging? Do you get high blood pressure at a certain time of the month, or when you're around a certain group of people? If so, make an active decision to combat these patterns.

6. **Talk.** Discuss your turmoil and troubles with a trusted friend or your partner. They can offer their perspective and opinions, and a problem shared is a problem halved.

7. **Walk.** Change your scenery; get out of a bad environment. Even if you can escape for only five minutes, leave your desk or your flat and take a walk around the block and get some fresh air.

8. **Spray some scent.** A new aroma can transport your stressed-out self to a better place. Lavender is calming, lemon is refreshing and re-energising, whereas vanilla can take you back to childhood. Keep some oils and sprays handy in those places where you often find yourself stressed.

9. **Stretch.** Wake up your body with a few limb exercises. I love clasping my hands together and pulling as far forward as possible and holding, then clasping behind the back, pushing up, and holding. This stretches out an achy back.

10. **Have a hot bath.** This is a simple measure, but, boy, does it feel good. Light some candles, grab your favourite book and hide in some bubbles for as long as you want!

Learning to switch off

You can't live for your boss, and you can't live in the office – however much your inner organised diva is telling you to be at their beck and call 24/7. You also can't get yourself worked up and frustrated when your boyfriend can't find his socks or lets down his friends (more on troublesome boyfriends in Chapter 8). Here are some chill-out guidelines:

◆ **Use all your allotted holiday.** The company won't pay you extra to sit at your desk. Plan your diary to take maximum time off!

◆ **Keep some days special.** If Saturday is the day you normally spend with your partner, let only very important things come in the way.

◆ **Oops, your mobile phone has run out of battery.** Enjoy it.

◆ **If you're taking a week off and planning a trip,** hand over all work to your colleagues, and make sure you're home/pets/plants are being cared for, so that you can totally forget about your normal, everyday life.

◆ **When away from the office,** don't watch TV shows related to your employment if they remind you of work, and don't read books on related subjects either.

◆ **Start your free time** (or get over a horrific day) by treating yourself to a massage or pedicure. You deserve it.

NB Don't become too anally retentive! There's being organised, and there's being a type-A totally demented army captain. Chill out. Let some things go. No one likes someone who is too strict or has lost all sense of fun. When I get too serious or wound up, I flick through photo albums of teenage parties or fantastic holidays to remind me of how I used to be, or how I can be when given the chance.

Secrets of Success

◆ Remember your to-do list – there's no point doing one, and then leaving it at home or losing it entirely.

◆ Some people can really stretch out anything. Learn to be fast. When you've got a busy day, walk quicker, react quicker, go to your favourite place for lunch and order your usual, and so on. Don't waste time making decisions that don't matter.

◆ If you want to get things done quicker: daydream less, physically do more. It's that simple.

◆ If you have a friend who is always late, don't sit around wasting your own time waiting for them. Good-naturedly tell them you're aware of their character flaw – and you're going to arrive for any meeting half-an-hour late yourself from now on. They'll think you're joking – but you might both end up getting there at the same time from now on!

◆ Another de-stressor is to de-clutter. Be it your home or your desk, or even your handbag, there is something soothing about getting these areas in order. It gives you a clean perspective.

◆ If you can feel yourself going from organised to totally organised, to an anally retentive nut job, seek help. Go to a farm in the middle of nowhere, with no make-up or phone, and practise yoga for a week.

Chapter Two

Wardrobe wonders and beauty secrets

Wʜᴀᴛ ɪꜱ ᴀɴ ᴏʀɢᴀɴɪꜱᴇᴅ mind with a disorganised appearance worth? Not very much – so a modern girl needs to learn how to pull it all together when it matters. Tracksuits and uggs are fabulous for cold, winter days, but sometimes a little more effort is needed.

How to organise your wardrobe

Unless you're in the envious position of having a large, luxurious walk-in closet to house all your outfits, then the chances are you're going to have to get smart with your space so that you don't end up with crushed clothes in your closet hanging haphazardly off hangers.

1. **Have a clear out.** First of all you need to get ruthless. It's worth investing the time to have a good sort through of what you have lurking in your wardrobe. Be honest, if it doesn't fit, or if you haven't worn it in the past year, throw it out. If you can't bring yourself to give everything away to the charity shop, then consider throwing a 'switch and bitch' party for your friends (a new craze: friends get together for a gossip and a drink, and swap unwanted items of clothing with friends – it's addictive!). Or, if even that is too traumatic, then at least put these clothes in a box and store them safely away. At least you'll know that if sequined hot pants ever come back into fashion, or if you do lose that 4.5kg (10lb) you've been meaning to, you can get your hands on them. Set yourself a deadline, though; if after a year you still haven't worn any of these clothes, now is the time to do your bit for charity.

2. **Organise by season.** Unless you're living the jet-set cosmopolitan lifestyle when you're frequently crossing hemispheres and seasons, then most likely you can divide

your wardrobe into at least two seasons: spring/summer and autumn/winter. Unless you've adequate room (see Storage below), then any out-of-season clothes should be stored away until an appropriate time.

> **JANE, 31**
>
> ❝I pack away clothes depending on whether it's spring/summer or autumn/winter – but I label the bags carefully for those emergency "I need sun breaks" that hit me every February ... I don't have to pull out bag after bag of summer work clothes, I just head straight for the bikini and sarong one!❞

3. **Storage.** Clothes should be hung on either shaped plastic, wooden or padded hangers. Never ever hang anything on a wire coat hanger – they can't take the weight of the garment and they'll damage the fabric or leave unsightly shoulder bumps. Delicate garments should be hung on padded hangers – they're expensive but they're worth the investment to keep your clothes looking better for longer.

- Clothes should be hung on a rail with at least 2.5cm (1in) between hangers. Squishing in too many clothes on the rail will only result in clothes becoming crushed and you looking dishevelled.

- If you have limited hanging space, then jumpers/sweaters and T-shirts can be folded and stored in a drawer. They may need a quick once-over with the iron to remove any folding creases before you wear them, but any creases in all-natural-fibre garments should fall out soon after wearing.

NB You can buy special plastic storage bags that you remove the air from at most large DIY stores. Simply fold up your clean clothes and secure the bag before sucking out the air with the vacuum cleaner. You'll be amazed by how much the size of the bag and contents will shrink! And the bags will keep your clothes dust- and cat-hair-free until you are ready to use them again.

Coordination clues

It's not just about the dress or the coat – there are so many other things to think about, too.

Undercover story

Of course, any modern girl like you will only wear matching sets (remember ladies, when buying new underwear, purchase two pairs of matching knickers to any bra, as you can invariably get two days out of a bra before washing). To avoid spending precious time in the morning rummaging through your underwear drawer, try threading your knickers through a fastened bra to keep them together. These can then be folded and stored carefully. If you keep your matching sets only for those occasions when they might get a public display then I hope you're at least wearing colour-coordinated underwear. (Tip: to keep lacy or delicate underwear looking good you'll have to wash it by hand; sorry, there's no other way around this!)

Shoe fetish

Every girl's favourite accessory can be stored on a rack or, if you don't have enough space, then stacked in shoeboxes at the bottom of your wardrobe. A nice idea is to take a

Polaroid photo of each pair and stick it to the front of the box. An easier and just as effective way, though, is simply to write a description on the side of each box, or buy the see-through boxes, if you can find them.

Bedazzled

Jewellery and accessories are a key part of any modern woman's wardrobe and can often make an outfit. Treat yourself to a jewellery box that displays all your jewellery to save you precious moments searching for a matching earring. Silver tarnishes and diamonds can lose their sparkle; make sure you regularly clean your jewellery to keep it looking its best. A trip to a jeweller can help keep expensive items looking fabulous as it's worth having expensive jewellery professionally cleaned. If you've lots of costume jewellery, then storing it in a cutlery tray inside a drawer can be an effective way of keeping everything in its place and easy to hand.

LOUISA, 28

6 I keep my jewellery draped around my bedposts – necklaces on one and bracelets on the other. Not only does it look good, and hey it's cheap decoration, but also I never forget to put it on when I leave for the day. I never forget what I own, because it's there right in front of me – and not too far away from my wardrobe, so I can see what matches. 9

Belt up

If you're tight for space, belts can be hung on the back of a wardrobe door. Take a trip to a DIY store and buy some hooks that can easily be affixed with nails or even adhesive pads.

Bag lady

Every woman knows that the right bag is key to any outfit. Don't be misguided into thinking you need a new bag every season in every colour, though. The most smartly dressed women invest in a maximum of one or two designer bags. Choose leather – it'll last much longer and looks better and better with age. Be practical: there's no point in buying the little clutch even if you've fallen head over heels in love with it, if you're the kind of girl who likes to cart around the kitchen sink with her. If you're only going to buy one bag, choose wisely. Tan leather goes with black and brown; cream leather can also work really well with most colours and for most seasons.

How to get ready in a hurry

I'm so jealous of celebrities whose main occupation is to look gorgeous. They're not like us! Forget rushing into work at some ungodly hour with your party frock in a plastic carrier bag and a few items of make-up shoved in the desk drawer to turn you into Cinderella after nine hours of hell in the workplace. They get to wake up leisurely, and, after a healthy breakfast, head to the gym or the spa, and then, with the help of a stylist, pick a perfect outfit and get their hair done for any important meeting or event. But, back in the real world, we battle on and do the best we can.

The office

The key to getting ready in a hurry for any occasion is to rely on a few key wardrobe staples. Depending on the dress code in your office these may be:

- A well-fitting smart suit in a neutral colour (black or brown are the most practical and flattering).

- A pair of classic, well-tailored trousers (flat-fronted and wide-legged suit most body shapes best).

- A white shirt (starched and immaculately ironed!).

- A tailored skirt in a neutral block colour (A-line or pencil, depending on your preference, are classic styles and never date. A-line suits fuller hipped girls; pencil is fab for lucky slim people).

- A woollen (but preferably cashmere if you can afford it) jumper or cardigan – choose a flattering colour for your skin tone (more on this in a bit)

The perfect capsule wardrobe contains only a few key pieces in neutral colours; interest is added by the use of accessories – a silk scarf, or interesting necklace, for example. You can wear the same basic things every week and just spice them up with added bling. Keep everything colour-coded and simple, clean and neat, and you'll cut your 'Oh what shall I wear to that meeting?' panic time in half. And you know what that means? More time in bed in the morning!

The party

This is where those sparkly, dangly diamond earrings really come into their own! Sparkle really dresses up any outfit and helps make the transition from day to night. If you can carry it off, slick some glitter lipgloss over your lipstick for added glamour, or a quick sweep of shiny eye shadow can work wonders.

- You can never go wrong with a little black dress with black stilettos, and fishnets in cold weather. It's a cliché but the right LBD can really take you anywhere. If you work in an office, then consider investing in a black shift dress; it can work for day with a simple pair of heels and a cardigan, but can easily transform into the perfect party outfit with a change of accessories.

- Well-fitting jeans and a sexy top are easy to commute in, easy to get drunk in, and not too OTT.

- One on-trend piece (look at fashion magazines for the colour, fabric or shape of the moment, you don't have to spend a fortune – just head to your high street for cheap but good stuff!).

- Get a fabulous frock coat that can be thrown over the most plain and dull work outfit. I have a sparkly Russian peasant coat (which sounds hideous, I know) but I can chuck it over pyjamas when I'm walking to get coffee in the morning and everyone thinks I look fabulous!

NB Finding the right shades to wear is important so consider making an appointment with a 'colour consultant' to help you find the most flattering colours for your skin tone. The wrong shade of pink can leave you looking tired and washed out, whereas the perfect tone can lift and mask tiredness. You'll be given a book of perfect tones to suit your skin, bring out the best in you, and visually slim you down!

How to look after your clothes and accessories

Hems fall down; buttons fall off – but don't panic! There's no need to be a qualified seamstress to learn a few basics in clothes maintenance. Ask your most wonderfully groomed friend to show you how, if you really don't know. Here are five easy tips to keep you neat and wonderful:

1. When you buy new clothes, they frequently come with a spare button or two attached to the label. Keep these safe – they will be used one day! Buy yourself a small photo album (one of those where you slip the photos into clear plastic pockets) and store spare buttons in there, together with a description of the item of clothing they came from.

2. Undertake repairs as soon as they are needed. The day will soon come when you're rushing to get ready for work only to find your favourite suit is missing a button.

3. If a hem comes down and you're in a hurry, use some iron-on 'magic invisible hem': it's quick, easy, and does the job.

4. The next time you're staying in a hotel, take the freebie sewing kit and store it in your purse – you never know when you'll have a wardrobe malfunction.

5. Heels and soles should *always* be maintained with regular trips to the cobbler. There is no surer way to cheapen an otherwise nice outfit than by wearing run-down heels; it just shouts 'Slob!'. Another no-no while we're on the subject is leaving price labels on the soles of your shoes – no, no, no!!!

NB When doing your laundry, don't cut corners to save time or to save doing an extra wash (even if you feel it's time-consuming!). Follow the washing instructions on care labels carefully. Learn what the different symbols mean. 'Cold wash' means just that: cold, not 40 degrees, unless you want to risk shrinkage. Don't leave 'dry clean only' garments to fester at the bottom of your laundry bin. Why not organise a weekly drop-off/collection with your local dry cleaners?

Beauty secrets of busy women

When you're worried about spending enough time with your boyfriend, or planning ahead for your next high-powered business presentation, worrying about your looks can seem pretty petty and vacuous – but hey, you don't want to be the ugly one in any scenario. Grooming, girls, grooming – it's never a waste of time!

Find a good beautician

Locate someone whom you like and trust – and then hang on to her! A good beautician is worth her weight in gold. Tip her and she'll help you out of last-minute panics when you suddenly get an invitation for a weekend at the beach a week before your next waxing appointment.

Appointments

Make regular appointments for all your must-do maintenance work: eyebrow shaping, waxing, and so on. This way you'll make sure you get regularly de-fuzzed every five or six weeks and you'll keep looking groomed at all times. Set these appointments in stone, the same way you would keep to a business meeting. A regular facial should be considered 'maintenance' rather than a once-in-a-while luxury. Regular exfoliations and blackhead extractions will keep your skin clear and glowing. If you can't afford to head to a spa, DIY at home. Invest in some good scrubs and spot creams, and make time once a week – even if it's in the shower and completed in one minute – to take care of your skin. Dead skin cells equal a dull complexion – and who wants that?

Express yourself

Express beauty bars are springing up on every high street and they're perfect for the busy modern woman who receives a last-minute invitation to a hot party or a mini-break. A quick paint-and-polish manicure is a fast way of instantly giving your hands a groomed finish. And in the summer, painted toes should always accompany open-toed sandals.

Another timesaver is to get someone to come to your office or home. Travelling beauty gurus are becoming more and more widespread, so you can get plucked and pruned and perfected while babysitting at home or answering phone calls in the office!

Magical multitasking

The best-groomed busy modern women know how to multi-task – and their beauty regime is no exception! Put a hair treatment on your head before you paint your nails so that this can take effect while you're waiting for your nails to dry. Meanwhile, use the time wisely to squeeze in a few facial exercises to tone your face and neck muscles, or squeeze in a few pelvic floor exercises (they're not only for pregnant women – your boyfriend will also feel the benefit!).

Gym-bunny benefits

Make the most of your gym facilities to get groomed quickly. Use their fancy products if they have them, or at the very least keep an exfoliator and razor with you to use your post-workout shower time wisely. Take a deep-conditioning hair treatment with you to put on in the sauna or steam room; it will work at double speed in the heat.

SARAH, 35

❛My mother and I have turned getting groomed into a social event. We used to get together once a month to catch up and moan about our other halves over lunch and a bottle of Merlot, but now we meet at her house and Julie – a beautician who has just left a salon and set up a mobile business on her own – comes over and sorts us out. While I'm getting my lashes and brows tinted, my mum's toenails are drying, etc. So we still catch up and stay close, but get more beautiful at the same time, too!❜

Making the most of your beauty sleep

A modern girl – even an organised one – doesn't always have time for the recommended eight hours' beauty sleep, so here's how to cheat and wake up looking like you've been tucked up in bed all night:

◆ ALWAYS remove your make-up before going to bed. It doesn't really matter how; use whatever works for you, but just make sure you do it! Leaving it on will block pores, and that causes spots.

◆ Apply a good moisturiser. Skin can get dehydrated in the night, leaving fine lines on your skin. A good moisturiser will help your skin keep hydrated and plump out those fine lines.

◆ Hands are one of the first places where ageing is most evident. Keep your hands looking young and soft by applying a thick moisturiser before bed and wearing cotton gloves to bed. The same can be said for feet (although substitute the cotton gloves for socks unless you have toes like a primate!).

◆ Slick some lip balm onto your lips before retiring to bed. This will help you avoid dry, cracked lips on waking and ensure your lipstick goes on smoothly.

◆ To wake up with a golden glow, apply fake tan before going to bed. There's nothing like the look of sun-kissed skin to make you glow with health and vitality!

◆ If you know you're not going to have time for a hair wash and blow-dry in the morning, try sleeping with your hair in plaits. It works best on hair that hasn't been washed for two to three days and you'll wake up with lovely curls and volume.

◆ If you can feel a pimple emerging, go to bed with tooth-paste on the zit zone, or a strong perfume dabbed there. These will dry out the problem area and should halt an eruption; otherwise, they will bring it to a head – so to speak – to make it easy for removal without digging and squirming, and the threat of scarring.

Perfect hair on the quick

Maintaining good hair need not take hours and hours:

1. To start with, be honest with your hairdresser and de-mand an easy hairstyle, one with little maintenance. Remember that hair trimmed every two months is easier to maintain than dry, unmanageable hair.

2. If your roots are coming through, ask your salon to high-light just the front and parting – you only have to do a full head of colour twice a year.

3. If your hair looks greasy, just wash the front and fringe, and blow-dry. Or use a dry shampoo, which is available from all good chemists. Just be careful to brush through properly to avoid that 'dusty' look.

4. If you're hair is a tangly mess in the morning, use a leave-in conditioner. Comb through and leave to dry naturally – this is especially good for curly hair.

5. Save time when blow-drying by pinning the hair into sections and focusing on one bit at a time. This might seem time-consuming but it actually dries the hair much quicker.

Secrets of Success

◆ For your outfits, stick to three colours that suit you, and which can be easily mixed and matched. Black, white and yellow are a fabulous combo for blondes; black, brown and red for brunettes; green, grey and blue for redheads. This will save time when you delve into your wardrobe each morning.

◆ Keep your most-worn shoes and coats in the hallway, stored neatly on hooks and in boxes.

◆ If you're having a bad hair day, don't fret or go to the office in a sombrero. Try a ponytail. They're fashionable and easy to do. Make it smarter by wrapping a section of hair from underneath the tail around the elastic band and fasten with a clip underneath.

◆ If you're short of time getting ready for a night out, just focus your attention on one area when it comes to make-up – your eyes or your lips, not both. And always apply make-up in good light, or you will see yourself in a different mirror and need to redo it!

◆ Tinted lip balms are conditioning and look good – and easy to apply in a hurry (even without a mirror).

◆ Get your eyelashes and brows tinted to save time, and investigate a good eyeliner semi-permanent tattoo, if you usually wear lots of eye make-up.

◆ When you don't have time to redo your pedicure or manicure, just reapply a topcoat of a high-gloss polish in the same or a similar shade. Gloss hides minor imperfections.

◆ If you're really feeling pale or peaky, applying blusher to the apples of your cheeks is the quickest way to look perky. If you have an extra 30 seconds, wake up your eyes with a quick dab of highlighter just below your brow bones.

◆ Fake tan is the quickest look-good-and-thin quick tip. Go bronze!

Chapter Three

How to keep a happy home

HOME REALLY IS WHERE the heart is, so when you get the time to spend time there you should be able to enjoy it rather than stressing about completing chores, tidying the garden or doing the laundry. This chapter offers shortcuts to domestic bliss.

Fabulous food

My dad says I live to eat (I enjoy stuffing myself and trying new things so much), whereas he eats to live (he just tops up his energy levels to get him around a golf course). Whichever category you fall into, having good food to offer guests – and yourself after a hectic day – is a major part of home organisation.

Housekeeping tips for the weekly shop

This is one area where you really can't be slapdash – or you'll have to run back to the shops for something you've forgotten!

◆ Don't go shopping without a detailed list.

◆ Think hard of all the main meals you're planning for the week ahead. Plus, think about packed lunches to take for work if you're that organised, too!

◆ If you live with a man, try to find out when he's out or away during the week, as you won't need to buy as much! And you can eat what you like and have lazy, girly dinners of egg and soldiers/baked beans on toast/scrambled eggs/salads/dips and baguette.

◆ Think of what you will cook each day and buy the necessary ingredients. Plus, remember the basics: milk, juice, butter or margarine, bread, fruits and veg.

◆ Keep your shopping list where the whole family can find it and tell them to write down items they have taken from the store cupboard: everything – from lightbulbs to choc biscuits, loo paper to teabags, including things that usually don't need to be bought weekly but are a total pain if you run out.

◆ While shopping, check dates! Remember: goods to the back of supermarket fridges tend to have a longer life. Why buy eggs with a shelf life of one week when you can reach to the back and buy eggs with a life of three weeks?

◆ Take advantage of the three-items-for-the-price-of-two offers on goods you use all the time. As long as you have storage space – and the dosh – it's crazy not to buy. However, don't be tempted to shell out on goods that you are less likely to use. This especially applies to fruit and veg. It might work out that it is only a small amount more to buy a whole bag of pears instead of only one – but will you be able to eat them before they go rotten?

◆ Don't just stick to buying food in supermarkets. They are now great places to find clothes, stationery, books and CDs.

◆ Most supermarkets now have shopping on-line. All seem to work well. Just be aware that although they won't send you anything out of date, if you do the shopping yourself, you could do better! However, this is still a great time-saving service for working girls and busy mums.

HELEN, 40

❝ It's worth just spending five to ten minutes once a week to think about what main meals you'll have for the next seven days. Sit with a diary so that you can take into account which members of the family will be around for each meal. For example, if my teenage son James isn't around we'll have fish, as he won't touch it! Then, with a list, I'll buy the week's main meal food on one shopping trip. Without a list, you will forget things. It doesn't matter if you come back with extras, but it's such a pain if you forget essentials. ❞

Keep it fresh

It goes without saying that's it's healthy (and you feel so worthy) to buy as much fresh produce as possible. Fresh veg is just so quick to prepare and cook, and chicken or fish can be cooked in under half an hour if grilled or fried. If you're too tired to cook properly, make good use of eggs – they can be cooked in all kinds of very quick ways – and drink milk (the perfect food!). Just always make sure you eat the minimum of five fruits and veg a day, which may sound a lot but it's easy once you're in a routine. I start every morning with a freshly juiced concoction of carrot, apple, orange and spinach – four in one! Make good use of ready-prepared salads and veggies, which are stocked by most supermarkets, but do remember: if a rapidly changing work and social schedule means you're throwing the contents of your fridge away week after week, stock up on frozen veg. They have been proven to be just as good nutritionally (nearly!).

NB Life is much simpler if there are no chocs/crisps/ goodies in the house – for obvious reasons. You'll binge in a weak moment and then spend a few hours moaning and groaning about your fat ass and lack of willpower. Who needs that? If you have men and/or kids around, stock up on a sweet thing that you can resist. I don't like ice cream, for example, so the freezer can be full of that and I won't care, however pre-menstrual I am!

The perfectly stocked fridge

The huge American-style fridges of today are used as larders 'of old' were: for storing preserves and sauces, bread and cakes, bottled waters and squashes. However, most of these don't actually *need* to be kept cold.

Essential items that *do* need to be kept cool are:

eggs

milk

marge and butter

some cheeses (check the packaging)

cold meats and bacon

fresh fish and poultry

All of the above, with the exception of milk, have a remarkably long life if kept cool, and milk can be stored in the freezer if skimmed or semi-skimmed. And, most importantly, quick and nutritious meals can be thrown together from the above ingredients.

Quick and foolproof recipes

When you've spent a day at work, you won't have the time or inclination to get all Gordon Ramsay – I doubt! So learn where to cut corners and use a few useful recipes (see below) that you can make do with your eyes closed. Always take full advantage of ready-made sauces, and so on. Just cook meat (chicken or beef mince are popular favourites), add sauce, and off you go. Serve with potatoes and veg, pasta or rice. They are all so very easy, tasty and nutritious if done correctly.

There are lots of cookbooks around that concentrate on very simple recipes. Investigate them – Jamie Oliver and Delia Smith are particularly good for this. The best kind of simple recipes have very few ingredients and don't take long to throw together. Here are some of my favourite, simplest, tastiest time-lifesavers! Use all three together for an easy to prepare mid-week dinner party!

COLOURFUL SOUP (IT'S DELICIOUS!)

Ingredients • SERVES 4

115g (4oz) butter

1 round lettuce, cut into fine strips

800g (1lb 12oz) frozen petits pois

10ml (2 tsp) salt

5–10ml (1–2 tsp) sugar

ground black pepper

1 litre (1³/₄ pints) cold water

1 Melt the butter in a saucepan, and put in the lettuce. Add the peas, salt, 5ml (1 tsp) sugar and pepper.

2 Cover the pan, and cook gently for 10 minutes.

3 Add the water and cook until the peas are tender. Taste, adjust the seasoning and add more sugar if necessary.

4 Purée in an electric blender. Return to the pan and heat through. Serve.

SIMPLE SMOKED HADDOCK (SUPERB!)

Ingredients • SERVES 4

25g (1oz) unsalted butter

15ml (1 tbsp) olive oil

1 garlic clove, sliced

4 thick haddock or cod fillets, about 175g (6oz) each

a little chopped parsley (optional)

the zest of 1 small lemon

1 Heat the butter, olive oil and garlic in a large pan over a medium heat until the mixture starts to foam and sizzle.

2 Put the fish into the pan, skin-side down, and fry over a high heat for 10 minutes – this will give a golden crust underneath the fish.

3 Turn the fish over and scatter over the parsley, if using, and lemon zest. Fry for a further 30 seconds. Put each cooked fillet onto a warmed plate and spoon over some of the buttery juices. (Serve with soft poached eggs or green veggies – and a glass of chilled white wine!)

LEMON ICED PUD (EVERYONE'S FAVOURITE!)

Ingredients • SERVES 4

225g (8oz) digestive biscuits

juice and zest of 2 lemons

175g (6oz) sugar

large can evaporated milk, chilled

1 Put the biscuits in a food processor and pulse to make crumbs. Alternatively, put them in a plastic bag and roll over the biscuits with a rolling pin.

2 Mix the juice and zest of the lemons with the sugar and leave to stand for 30 minutes.

3 Meanwhile, whip the chilled evaporated milk until thick. Stir the sugar mixture and the milk together.

4 Put a layer of the creamy lemon mixture into a freezer-proof bowl. Add a thin layer of crushed digestive biscuits. Continue in this way until all the mixture is used up.

5 Freeze until solid. Remove from the freezer and transfer to the fridge 1 hour before serving to allow the mixture to soften.

THE PERFECT CAKE

If you want to get all Domestic Goddess, or impress your mother-in-law, here is the cake for you – it's impossible to get wrong and is so easy and quick to do! This recipe makes a small cake, so I usually make double for a larger cake or make two cakes to save time – it's just as easy and you can pop one in the freezer (perfect for emergencies)! You can choose your baking tin according to how you want to serve it: a loaf tin (for slicing), square (for cutting into fingers) or traditional round if you want to present it iced and pretty.

Ingredients • SERVES 4

175g (6oz) butter or margarine

140g (5oz) soft brown sugar

350g (12oz) mixed dried fruit

200g (7oz) crushed pineapple (use canned and crush in a blender)

3 eggs, beaten

200g (7oz) self-raising flour, sifted

a little milk, if necessary

1   Preheat the oven to 140°C/275°F/Gas 1. Grease and line a 20cm (8in) round or square cake tin or a 680g (1½lb) loaf tin with baking parchment. Put the butter or margarine, sugar, dried fruit and pineapple in a saucepan and bring to the boil. Let it simmer for five minutes then leave to cool slightly.

2   Add the beaten eggs and flour, and mix well. The mixture should drop off the spoon easily – if not, add a little milk. Transfer the mixture to the prepared tin.

3 Bake for about 1½ hours or until firm in the centre and a skewer inserted into the centre comes out clean. Leave to cool in the tin for five minutes, then turn out of the tin and cool on a wire rack. When cool, wrap in foil and leave for a few days (anything up to a week). This makes the cake lovely and moist, and easy to cut.

The perfect property

There really is no place like home. After a gruesome day in the office and a hellish commute there's nothing quite like going through your own front door, flopping on the sofa with a cup of tea (or glass of wine, if it has been a really tough day) and taking pleasure from your home comforts. Here are a few clues to making your home even more homely.

House proud

Housework is horrid and boring, and very few people genuinely enjoy it. It is constant and monotonous and you can never ever really get on top of it. Dust keeps landing, laundry keeps arriving, toilets keep needing to be cleaned, and so on, but you can make life easier for yourself from the start:

◆ **Avoid dark carpets.** They show so much dirt and dust. Believe it or not, beige or light brown is best. A carpet with a fleck is even better because it helps to disguise any stains/dirt/dust that appear. A dark carpet could be hoovered in the morning and look less than perfect by the evening (through normal family use) – with beige types, however, you can get away with hoovering once a week.

- ◆ **Avoid dark furniture.** It shows dust incredibly. Light furniture is much more practical and needs less dusting.

- ◆ **Multitask when dusting.** Catch up on phone calls with girlfriends. Use one of those specially manufactured large fluffy mitts that actually soak up the dust. (Normal dusting sends dust back into the air and it lands again an hour or so later.)

- ◆ **Do chores in the correct order.** Change sheets and then dust, hoover first and then dust. (Both changing bed linen and vacuuming cause dust, so if you dusted first you'd be undoing all your work!)

Bathrooms

These must be kept clean and sanitary looking. Everyone hates a dusty, grimy bathroom and what is worse than a filthy loo? Nothing. Yuk! To save yourself from a real build-up of nastiness, every time you use the shower or bath, or wash in the basin, spend two minutes wiping down after yourself – especially after cleaning your teeth, when toothpaste gets everywhere and gels to the side of the basin. Rub vigorously all around the shower, bath or basin, and if there is no cloth handy, use your dirty towel or even an item of clothing you took off before washing. We are not talking about if the bathroom is filthy here, just if damp and smeary and soapy – and the towel/clothes are going straight into the wash basket, aren't they? Get in the habit of leaving the bathroom clean behind you.

As for dirty loos – there's no excuse. Invest in a good, hard loo brush and use it if ever anything is left behind, and encourage your housemates to do the same. A liberal splash of good old-fashioned bleach gets rid of the most horrid stains, too. Be careful you don't get bleach on you, the surrounding flooring or anything else, however – it ruins everything.

Once a fortnight, remove everything from the surfaces, and give everything a good spray with a specially made bathroom cleaner. Leave it on for three minutes, and then polish off till you can practically see your face on everything. And don't forget to clean the mirror, too – vinegar on newspaper brings up a lovely smear-free shine.

Kitchen

Help yourself by keeping work surfaces as clear as possible. If you must indulge in ornaments, save them for the sitting room. Dust has a funny way of gathering around knick-knacks. If cleared of toot, kitchen work surfaces are easier to keep clean and look more like a serious workplace. Keep on top of dirt in the kitchen by giving a quick wipe down of the surfaces at least once a day and, unless seriously short of time, a quick once over on the floor with a mop covered by a throwaway floor wet-wipe.

Remember: unless you are careful, there are more germs on a kitchen chopping board than a toilet seat. Use different chopping boards for different produce – you can get food poisoning from using the same board to chop raw meat, if you then use it for cooked meat and vegetables. Be careful. A generous splosh of bleach or disinfectant and boiling water cleans germs from chopping boards easily and quickly. Throw old bits of food and waste away in the bin; don't leave it on surfaces.

NB There are companies who come in and professionally clean your oven for you – and this is a job few people relish. For a reasonable amount, these people leave your oven grand spanking new – and not a chemical smell around. Those spray-on oven cleaners you buy in the supermarket do work (after a load of scrubbing on your part!) but stink the kitchen out, make your eyes water and can make you wheeze, they are so loaded with goodness-knows-what. Treat yourself – get a man in! I do it twice a year. Oo-er! Money well spent and the oven truly looks brand new.

Laundry

Moan, grumble, yawn – this is my least favourite chore! Here is the most efficient way to cope with dirty clothes (other than racking up a huge dry-cleaning bill which, I know, is very tempting!).

- Divide the laundry according to colour first: if there's enough laundry, divide it into whites, darks and pastels (if less laundry, just whites and colours will suffice).

- Gather all your whites together and wash them in the lowest temperature recommended on all the garments. Therefore, if you have a white shirt (wash 60 degrees), T-shirt (40 degrees) and baby's jumper (woollen wash) bung all the whites in together and wash on the woollen wash. Don't worry about separate washes for clothes of different recommended temperatures. You'll be there all day. Think of the quickest route every time!

- The same goes for your coloureds. Use the safest warm wash. Jeans won't get damaged in a 30-degree wash (and with today's detergents they will be clean, so don't worry about that) but you can ruin a delicate fabric on a 50-degree wash.

◆ Don't kill yourself doing lots of wash loads in one day – unless you positively want to! Just keep your washing ticking over nicely by doing a wash load once you have enough to fill a washing machine, whether that is daily or once a week.

Windows

These are tricky to clean. Why else do you think there are so many professional window cleaners about? Despite the best of intentions, loads of elbow grease and really putting your back into it, somehow windows can end up worse than when you started. They look OK at first and then at the first glint of sunshine they look a grim, smeary mess. Despite all the products for cleaning windows in the supermarkets, probably the best thing to use is clean warm water with just a dash of washing up liquid. Wring out a cloth, give the window a darn good rub and then shine it off with a dry cloth. Nothing is really better.

But of course the best thing to do is to cheat! Get your local, friendly window cleaner to come indoors and clean your windows for you, just offer to double his payment. He's the real expert and makes it look effortless. Just remember to clear all your ornaments off the windowsill first! Even if you do this only once a year it's wonderful and a real treat for those windows. This is especially true if you have a conservatory.

Making it fun

If you hate all housework, make yourself do one chore in a 15-minute burst of high activity. If you hate hoovering, set yourself a time challenge. Start hoovering and look at your watch – tell yourself you'll stop after 15 minutes. Start with the areas that need hoovering most and it's amazing how much can be achieved with 15 minutes of vigorous activity. But don't stop there – once you've finished that, go on to something else for 15 minutes, because broken into short bursts like this, housework seems bearable. If you keep going for an hour, completing four different chores, you'll get through masses – and then the best bit is taking a guilt-free hour-long break just for you, straight afterwards. Sit with your feet up, make that coffee, read that glossy magazine or watch TV.

Another pleasant trick is to do chores listening to your iPod. Choose your favourite upbeat album or talking book, and off you go – you are entertained as you work. Catch up with all those TV shows you recorded on your video while you iron or prepare veggies for the night's supper. To make housework less painful:

◆ Don't become a slave to housework, but try to hoover at least once a week.

◆ Try to remove dust as it appears. As long as a place is reasonably tidy it will look OK. Don't beat yourself up if the house is not immaculate.

◆ Windows look lovely if they are bright and shiny, but the first fall of rain spoils them again. If you've cleaned them and they are spoiled, who cares? Tackle them again next month.

Family life

Keeping a house neat and tidy, and getting meals on tables, isn't made easier by having family around, but catch a break by doing the following:

◆ Keep a shopping list in a place that the whole family knows about. Whenever they open a new packet of anything, get them to write it on the list so that you can replace it on your next shopping trip. If they don't, it will impact on them when you run out of shampoo, breakfast bars, cola etc., even if they don't care about other items.

◆ It's really good manners – and practical – to expect children to ask before they help themselves to anything in the food line. It's not so much that you are going to refuse, it's just helpful for you to know how stocks are going down, and it does give you the opportunity to say no if it is too close to a meal time – or feel that the child has had too much junk that day.

◆ Give your children one chore a day that you know – and they know – they have to do. I grew up having to unload the dishwasher once a day. It seemed like the most evil thing in the world at the time, of course, but it didn't do me any harm – quite the opposite in fact.

◆ Expecting your mother or mother-in-law and no time to spare? Make sure you have a spray furniture polish that smells strongly of beeswax or some other smell associated with cleanliness, and then spend five minutes tidying up and then five seconds having a spray around.

Instant tips for making your home lovelier

Make your place somewhere you want to hang out in, and your friends want to visit.

Fresh air

There's nothing quite like it! It's certainly better than any artificial smells from fake air freshener. Houses can become stuffy and stale-smelling very quickly – and the most embarrassing thing is that the person who lives there does not notice. Every day, open every window. Even if bitterly cold outside and you can only open the window a crack. Even in the depths of winter if I'm alone in my home I open every window a tiny bit, and just get on with whatever I'm doing. As I go around the house and notice a room or hallway is too cold I then close the appropriate window. If very, very cold, all windows could be closed again within three minutes! However, it's amazing how if you are busy you don't particularly notice, and windows in some little-used rooms could remain open (just slightly!) for hours. In summer, there's no excuse for not opening windows. But for goodness sake, walk round and check they are all closed and locked again before going out!

Tidy up!

A tidy house is a calm house. The cleanest house in the world, if covered by a layer of general junk and debris, can look horrible and depressing (and embarrassing). It's amazing how just five minutes tidying the messiest room can make huge improvements – if the five minutes is used working steadily, not daydreaming! My best tip, though, is to tidy as you go along. If you have children, don't allow them to bring all their toys into your living area. And at the end of the day clear toys away (even if they are just chucked in a box behind the sofa), so that you can relax in front of the TV without toys all over the place.

Make your bed every morning. Nowadays with duvets there is no excuse. Yes, it is better to leave beds to air, but it's so much nicer to return to a room with a made bed – and a bedroom with a tidy bed looks 'straight' immediately. Messed-up bedclothes look untidy and are depressing. If you want to air your bed, fold down the duvet neatly and prop up the pillow against the headboard.

Storage space really aids tidiness. No handy cupboards? Can shelves be put up? Better to have crowded shelves than items left all over the place. Utilise every space – under the stairs, under the beds.

Encourage kids to help with general home tidiness. Be strict! It won't hurt them! Tell kids to tidy their things – and mean it. If everyone makes an effort it won't be too bad, but if no one makes an effort, it will be *bedlam*. Boyfriends/ husbands could fit into this category, too. Don't make yourself a doormat, girls, or those boys will walk all over you wearing dirty shoes. It's possible to make games out of work chores. Could you make 'helping Mum' part of the deal by which kids get spending money?

LINDA, 42

❝ Peeling vegetables at Christmas is a real drag – there are so many to do and I'd rather be drinking Bailey's looking at the Christmas tree! So a few years ago I invented the Harper Family Peeling Race. The kids – and my husband – love it, and they get so competitive peeling potatoes and carrots on Christmas Eve that they forget it's a chore and the job gets done in a quarter of the time. The winner gets a warm mince pie! ❞

Don't leave dirty washing lying about. Besides looking unsightly, some dirty washing smells (especially young males' pants, socks and T-shirts!). Especially make sure that no dirty underwear is lying around in bathrooms and bedrooms. Buy and use laundry baskets. No laundry basket? Then shove 'dirties' in a plastic supermarket carrier that can be tidied away.

Fresh flowers are lovely, but do need looking after. Water starts to smell after a couple of days if it is not changed regularly. If you don't have time to see to the flowers, don't buy them. Nothing looks sadder than old, worn, dried, unloved flowers in stinky old water (and they'll look like this in a few days in hot weather or with central heating). So, let fresh flowers be like chocolates: a real treat that others buy for you, and invest in some good-quality artificial flowers for everyday home brightening.

If at all possible, a 'real' fire is the ultimate luxury and makes any room more homely. There aren't many people who aren't drawn to a fire, but if you haven't got a real chimney, there are some fab flame gas fires around, so think about getting one fitted.

De-junk regularly. Try to clear out every cupboard, every drawer and every wardrobe each year. Sounds a doddle, but most of us won't achieve this; however, do try. Take every item out of one kitchen shelf or cupboard at a time. It'll be scary just how much food will be out of date. If you don't use that toasted sandwich/bread maker/juicer/steamer/ice-cream maker in a year, bin it or give it away. Not worn that jumper in a year? Bin that, too. De-junk all round the house. Anything that hasn't been used for a whole year? Ask the questions: is it beautiful? Has it got sentimental value? Can I live without it? (Bearing in mind you've already survived a whole year without touching it!) If still uncertain, stick it in a bin bag in the back of a cupboard.

You'll quickly realise you can live quite happily without it and can then let it go.

Persuading others to help you

Sadly for us modern girls, men are not psychic, and they may well not notice something that so obviously needs doing around the house. Let the steam coming out of your ears subside before asking your man to help, and remember to praise and say thank you afterwards – it works and he won't mind helping again. Don't suffer in silence, or sulk and get moody and bark, 'Nothing!' when they ask what is wrong – tell them. That is the best advice in the world where most husbands and boyfriends are concerned. Just remember they are hopeless at tuning into your brain, and they don't like playing guessing games. Spell out to them that you'd like them to wash up/play with the kids/tidy up, because they'll rarely guess on their own.

Another tip when asking friends or family for help is to ask the person well in advance (that is, if you need someone to babysit or for a lift somewhere). Normally, if you ask in plenty of time, people say yes without thinking, and it gives them time to plan around your needs. Make sure they write it down unless they have a super memory, and ring them a few days before to remind them.

It's hard to get kids to help because, basically, they see chores as a massive, er, chore! But we all hated it, too, didn't we? It's a pain, so we can see where they are coming from. In the long run, though, it does make their lives a little easier if they have met the odd chore before they go off to university or move out of home for whatever reason, so don't feel guilty about asking them. Teenagers come up with all kinds of reasons not to help (normally, home-work!), but try to be firm. Establish from an early age (maybe around six years old) that light chores are normal and part of family life, such as laying tables, putting dirty clothes washing in bins, attempts at bed making, attempts at tidying their rooms, keeping an eye on younger siblings while mum is out of the room. As they get bigger, cleaning cars, putting out the rubbish and the odd bit of gardening or shopping aren't outrageous requests. Remember: even if you are at home all day you are not doing your kids any favours by spoiling them and waiting on them hand and foot. They all have the time (if they want to find it) to help a little. Younger kids can be bribed and bigger kids threatened – they hate losing their pocket money!

JANE, 38

❝ Sometimes I have the time and inclination to be a "fun mummy" and play housewife with my young daughters. They love washing up, but I've discovered the hard way that it's not really wise to leave them on their own while doing it, for obvious reasons – flooding being one. Yes, they can help "with" cooking, but be prepared for the extra time required. Making chores into a race can work in short, sharp bursts. The child who first finishes tidying their room to a reasonable level gets a treat. Make a big thing about getting them all keyed up and shouting, "GO!" and off they go. But this won't work after a while – they aren't daft! By the way, if their rooms are in a really untidy state, accept the inevitable and do it yourself or get them to work alongside you. ❞

Green fingers

Just as a made bed has instant impact on making a bedroom look tidier, a mowed, neat lawn improves any garden immediately. So mow as and when necessary or, better still, instruct someone else to do it. This could be almost weekly in the summer months but less often in spring and autumn. Long, untidy grass looks awful and ruins the most beautiful garden. If you truly haven't got time to mow yourself, pay a local teenager to do it for you – or find a gardener. Mowing needn't be hard work. With the light hover-type mowers it's no bigger deal than hoovering. It's great if you can get that wonderful 'stripy effect' – but just neat and short will do! And don't forget the edges: they need to be trimmed, too! It's a pain going round with the shears, but tell your-self it can be done in 15 minutes maximum – and it can. Just switch on that iPod and shear to the music!

Apart from anything else, gardening is wonderful exercise. All that bending, reaching, lifting and pushing. And you could even be building up your tan. Plus, even on the dreariest day you'll get a glow in your cheeks. If you have kids, have them out in the garden with you. All that fresh air is marvellous for them. Toddlers can just toddle and babies can sit in their little chairs and watch – everyone benefits.

Once the lawn is under control, just generally neaten the flowerbeds, weed away and then cut back any plants that look overgrown. It is very hard to truly damage plants. They are very hardy and survive most things, including over-zealous attacks with the secateurs. Just cut plants back to a shape you like.

If you simply haven't got time to garden – and you can afford to do so – consider having the garden paved over, or cover it with shingle. This is often a more realistic compromise if you have a busy life and can't dedicate much time to your outdoor room! The children can cycle their bikes and bounce their balls on paving stones much easier than grass. It makes garden-lovers tut, but who cares! You don't have to justify to anyone what you do in your own garden. So straight away you are free from all the mowing and watering of lawn responsibilities.

Then invest in pots. For less work, have winter pots and summer pots. Stick bulbs in the winter ones and leave them there year in, year out. All bulbs seem to improve over the years with the one exception of hyacinths, so avoid them. Then have summer pots, filled with pansies, busy lizzies, marigolds or any plant that reseeds itself. These clever little plants will do the rest. Just resist the temptation to prod the bulbs during the summer or the newly seeded plants in the winter. The winter pots will look sad in the summer and the summer pots likewise in the winter – just stick them out of sight somewhere.

Gardening is great, as you can put in as much or as little effort as you like. As long as you do the basics that just keep the garden neat, it will be fine. If you really want to throw yourself in and spend hours out there, you'll reap the benefits of having a beautiful garden. There aren't many people who don't appreciate a nice, well-kept garden. Treat it as another room on your house. Don't let it become a horrible, nasty eyesore, a dumping ground for rubbish, old bikes, and so on.

Secrets of Success

◆ If you hate housework and can afford to, get a cleaner. There's nothing better than arriving home to find all the cleaning has been done! However, don't clean up for the cleaner – that's what you're paying the cleaner to do. But do tidy up before-hand – you don't pay out good money for someone to tidy up after you.

◆ Does the perfect home exist? The only comment I would make is that friends who have these wonderful beamed coun-try cottages say they are a pig to clean, so I suppose the answer has got to be that modern, easy-to-clean houses have their benefits, too – it depends how much work you want to put into your home.

◆ If you can't decorate, don't embark on it. Pay someone else to do it or bribe your dad/mum/brother or ex-boyfriend.

◆ If you can't afford much in your garden, get a gardener and ensure he or she does all the labour-intensive jobs, leaving you the pleasant ones such as dead-heading the flowers, and so on.

◆ Always clean garden tools when finished. Dirt left on will stick forever and make a job twice as long. Also, when planting, keep descriptive labels that come with plants all together in a box and refer to them later if necessary, instead of wasting time looking up the plants in gardening books. Don't throw them away or leave them on the plant itself, as the weather will cause the label to fade over time.

◆ Watering is a pain and it's time-consuming. So, if there's no hosepipe ban, install an irrigation system, available from your local DIY store.

◆ In the house, work methodically room-by-room, cleaning your most-used room first (so if interrupted, at least the important room's clean). Don't jump from one room to another and waste time.

◆ Did you know that cola is a very good loo cleaner? So, any left-over flat cola in tins or bottles can be poured down the loo (that makes two jobs in one: clean loo and disposal of cola!).

◆ We all need help – no one can do it all. Accept all offers of help graciously. When things go wrong in life, friends, family and neighbours often don't know what to say or do, but they often utter the words, 'If there is anything I can do ...' Well, tell them! If you need the kids picked up from school, or if it would be helpful if they picked you up a few things while they're at the supermarket, tell them. If, by chance, the offer of help was just empty words, you'll soon find out. They'll back out of granting your request or do it this time and simply not offer again. People aren't mind readers – so do tell them, and always say thanks.

Chapter Four

Getting your paperwork in order

Welcome to dullsville. There is no denying that even the most sadistic organiser can take no pleasure in paperwork and the hassle it brings. This chapter aims to bring you quick tips and time-saving solutions so that, with luck, you don't ever have to think too much about it again!

The joys of filing

When it comes to the joys of filing, there aren't any. Except that when done properly you never have to go through that gut-wrenching moment of panic when you can't find your birth certificate. Now, I'm not the best filer, but I do have three systems that I've learned work well:

Work filing

File work things according to project, person, year, and so on, of course. Plus, have a personal file where you keep things from home that need to be followed up during office hours, or which have been sent to your work email address. If buying a house or getting married, etc., it might be a good idea to keep a copy of all important personal documents filed at work so that they are easy to get hold of at all times.

> **ROSEMARY, 45**
>
> 6 My best advice for organising paperwork is to get one of those large briefcase things with the accordion-style files. This way you always have a place for each type of bill and statement. Get a new one each year and clearly write the date on the exterior so that everything is easy to find. Find-

> ing papers used to be a nightmare until I got one of these. Now I know where everything is and I don't let piles of paper or bills build up! **"**

Home filing

This consists of a series of boxes. If you're not neat enough or you don't have the room to put things under subjects in hanging files, these boxes are quick and easy to use and store (even under the bed, if it is high enough off the floor). Use one box as a 'memory box' where you can 'file' theatre tickets, photos you haven't yet put in an album, invites you haven't replied to yet and letters from friends, and so on. This is a fun box to look through on rainy Saturdays.

It's also important to have a 'serious' box, where you put every single bank statement, bill, legal document and employment contract. It's a good idea to open your post in the hallway and, after reading, lift up the lid and pop them in the appropriate filing box – if there's room to keep the boxes there. This way, things never get lost or damaged, and they are easy to revisit whenever the mood takes you!

PAYING BILLS ON TIME

If money's too tight to mention, staying in the black can be tough. Here are some helpful hints:

- If you can, ask all the different companies charging you to withdraw money the same day as you get paid.

- Try to pay all debts on the same day so that you don't get confused and miss a date.

- Set up as many repayments on direct debits as you can.

- If you share bill paying with someone else, set up a joint bank account to put money into and to take money out of. That way you can't get screwed by someone else's inability to get organised.

- Remember: it's not acceptable to pay bills late. You wouldn't like to get paid late, would you? It's the same thing – and of course you can incur nasty charges.

- If you can't set up a direct debit, keep all payment details saved in your phone or in your diary, so that you can pay over the phone in dead time such as queuing or commuting.

- Check your bank statements each month to make sure you have been debited the correct amount.

- If you simply can't pay bills because you don't have the money, take action fast. The solution is simple: cut back, you're spending more than you earn.

Important documents

Place super-duper important documents somewhere super-safe, like the places I mentioned above, and think about putting them in waterproof folders. It's also a good idea to take a few photocopies and distribute them around a number of places and people. If you happen to lose such a document, don't think, 'Oh well, I don't need it at the moment', and leave it, because these things can bite you on the arse. As soon as you realise, apply for a new copy, as it can take ages for a new one to arrive, and losing a passport, for example, can seriously affect travel plans.

Keep the contact phone numbers and addresses for all your important documents – such as passport, driving licence, visa papers – in your diary. You will then have them handy if anything gets lost, and you should update them when you move address or change your name.

When travelling, it is a good idea to keep photocopies of your passport and visa with you somewhere safe in case – God forbid – you lose them or they get stolen.

NB Digital cameras are fabulous, allowing self-editing so that we can all reach holiday-pose perfection, of course, but make sure you print out the photos! I think pictures are the most important life documents of all – capturing your loves, your ideals and your past. Too often now I hear 'Since I went digital, I don't have any photos printed out, and then I have to delete them because my memory card is full' grumbles. Well, stop being lazy and print. It is cheap and easy to do at any chemist or supermarket – and while you're at it, buy a photo album and file them away in date order, too. Call it a rainy-day project. I cannot tell you how many times over the years you'll get pleasure from doing this.

Finding the right bank in five easy steps

1. Only stick with your childhood bank if they value your custom and offer competitive services to stay.

2. Get paperwork on all the major banks and see who has the best interest rates and will offer you the best loans, services and someone to talk to rather than a robot, if ever you need to talk!

3. Internet banking is the way forward – and so easy. Find a bank that offers that service, as well as many accessible branches, to give you hands-on banking 24/7.

4. If you've had good treatment from your mortgage brokers or credit-card company, think about banking with them, too.

5. It's good to have a bank with branches near your office and your home – and with plenty of cashpoints that don't charge and are easy to use overseas.

SONIA, 32

❛ In January, I take advantage of my energy, my desire to be a better person, and the cold weather to really sort out all my paperwork from the year before. I look back over the last 12 months and sort my life out through pulp! I put photos away, I write down new addresses I've got from Christmas cards and cross out old ones. Plus, I add numbers I've started using, like the local pizza restaurant or dry cleaners, and transfer birthdays from my old calendar to the new one. I take a careful look at my receipts – and try to analyse where I spent too much money and where I could save some. I also think about how much money I've just spent on presents and feel guilty – so I research local charities and set up a direct debit for the next 12 months to help a little bit financially. ❜

Budgeting

As boring and serious as it sounds, having a clear budget outlining your income and expenditure will help you to control your finances and resist debt. To get to grips with your real budgeting cycle, make a record of your financial behaviour for one month – and I mean a record of everything you spend, not just a rough idea of socialising costs and the mortgage. (My big downfall is lunches and snacks at work. I can get through a fortune just on a few cappuccinos here and there, but it took a while to realise where my money was going.)

1. Once you have this sum in your head, divide your salary into 12 or look at your last three pay slips.

2. Add in extras that don't occur every month, such as buying Christmas presents, or taking your annual two-weeks' summer holiday.

3. If the difference between your income and expenditure is a positive amount, you have a budget surplus and that's great – this is the time to invest in shares or to open a high-interest savings account.

4. If you have a deficit, however, you need to change your spending habits to stop yourself from getting into debt. And there's no secret or sassy way to do this. You have to spend less.

Cost-cutting tips for the modern girl

◆ **Housing.** Take advantage of household items in the sales, and try to call in friends and family to do DIY for you, or pick up the paintbrush yourself rather than getting in a pricey handyman.

◆ **Transport.** Look after your car to save on repairs (go easy on the clutch, park it in a garage at night, if you have one, and so on) and use public transport where possible to save on petrol.

◆ **Food.** Eat breakfast at home before you go to work, and prepare your lunches to take with you. Use two-for-one offers and coupons at your favourite supermarket.

◆ **Clothing.** Shop for what you need, don't go shopping as a weekend recreational pastime. Try reading, exercising or hanging out with friends at the weekend instead of heading to the nearest shopping centre and its feast of temptations.

◆ **Entertainment.** Research your area to find out what activities are going on for free (local papers are great for this and there are always interesting, educational things happening), and do a few cheaper holidays this year rather than decadent long-haul ones.

◆ **Bills.** Shop around for the cheapest supplier for gas, water, electricity, insurance, satellite television, mobile phone, and so on. These are highly competitive markets and a different company will want to woo you away with a handsome offer.

Fitting in extra work to pay the bills

If you are still struggling financially after sensibly making as many cuts as you can, you may need to consider getting a second job. I have many friends who have done this when saving for a big event like a wedding or a year-long world trip, and although it's tough at the time, it's worth it not to have years of debt.

Look for a job that you can do at home at your pace first, be it making calls on behalf of a company or stuffing envelopes. You can also look for weekend work at your local supermarket or restaurant, or even consider late-night work stacking shelves – it sounds grim but, by all accounts, can be great fun.

Many modern girls take a less salubrious route and make easy money on sex phone lines or exotic dancing – both are growing industries. If you're morally able, and safe, I suppose it's worth thinking about. I'd find the former too laughable and the latter too diet-inducing, but different strokes (literally?) for different folks, hey? However you make your money, remember that this is to get yourself straight. Don't feel that because you've worked so hard you can treat yourself or treat it like toy money. And don't think you'll have to carry on working like a dog forever. All things will pass.

Splurging gone wild

We all love to splash out sometimes, and we all like to treat ourselves. But make sure you're not buying yourself stuff to make up for a gaping void in other areas. Lots of material needs are brought up by buried feelings of inadequacy, stress or depression. Every time you pull out your purse to buy an irrational item, think about why you need it, and will it really make you happy every time you wear it or use it, or are you just fulfilling a weird compulsion that should be sated elsewhere?

We all need to borrow at some point, but the only three really justifiable things to borrow for, in my mind, are a house, a car or urgent medical treatment. If you've run up huge credit-card bills because your partying is out of control and you're addicted to shoes, you need to change your ways fast. You should never borrow more money to get out of a debt problem, but you could shift who you are borrowing from to save on interest, and to get all your debts in one place so that they become more manageable. Talk to a financial advisor or search the Internet for official financial organisations to find out the best solution for your 'splashing-out regrets'. Don't keep your debt to yourself. It could become a dark and depressing secret. Talk to your family and plan a route of action. Most people have had tight times, so they won't judge you if you're honest.

Buying a property

Undoubtedly, the most important – and huge amount of paperwork – in your life occurs every time you buy a new property. There are important documents from lawyers, other people's lawyers, mortgage lenders, the council – it can be a nightmare. It's important to start a file immediately for all correspondence, and also to make a separate folder on your email to file all emails – both ones received and sent – as proof of agreed terms.

The process of buying is time-consuming and difficult, and it's crucial not to cut any corners – this will be the biggest investment of your life. Follow the guidelines below to make sure you tick all the boxes and ask all the relevant questions.

Where do you want to buy?

Don't just irrationally fall in love with a cottage you've seen in the property section of your local paper. Be sensible and organised, and think about the following. You will probably not be able to get the perfect place, but you need to tick as many boxes as possible. Make a list of all the things that are important to you, whether you want a house or a flat and how many bedrooms you desire. Then look at different areas to uncover:

1. How far it is from your work and what the local transport is like.

2. How far it is from friends and family (either far away or near can be a bonus, depending on your mindset).

3. The quality of nearby schooling, shops and restaurants.

4. The up-and-coming factor: is this area becoming more popular, therefore making it a good investment?

5. Is it overpriced? Are you getting less for your money than if you bought a property half a mile away, and do you care?

When you've found a property you're interested in buying, ask yourself:

1. Can you afford the upkeep? (Will it cost a lot to heat, tend the gardens, and so on?)

2. Is it in a noisy street?

3. What are the neighbours like?

4. Is there a garage and outdoor space?

5. Is it terraced, semi-detached or detached?

> **NB Never take the word** of the person trying to sell you the property alone – be it the vendor or the estate agent. They have a motive. Talk to the neighbours, other locals and read the local paper to get a real feel for the place. If it's in a different area, perhaps even spend a few nights out there to get the atmosphere.

Hounding estate agents

As soon as you've decided to buy somewhere, you must start chasing all the estate agents in the area you want to live in. Don't be loyal to one company – go for blanket coverage of them all. Then you have to write a time in your diary to call them at least twice a week, asking what new things have come up and if they have any new properties. This sounds silly because as they want to sell you something they should be chasing you, but, believe me, estate agents are only interested in you when there is a definite bite and they get their commission. It's your job to chase them.

When you are shown around properties, keep a record of each one so that you can compare and contrast as you go along. Make a note of good and bad points, and take a digital camera to snap away, if possible. Don't feel bad about asking for a second, third or fourth visit, or taking your dad or your builder friend round for an inspection – you're thinking about spending a lot of money.

Mortgage mayhem

As soon as you can, and before you've put an offer in, start searching around for the right mortgage. Repayments are normally the best, and easy for an organised girl who likes order in her life (you agree all terms and there is a pay-off date agreed and in sight unlike endowment mortgages which can backfire).

The amount you can borrow depends on your income, your deposit and your employment status. Other debts will also be taken into consideration. When choosing a mortgage, look for:

1. Does the mortgage offer guarantee a fixed rate of interest (and therefore monthly payment) for the first few years? This can help you to know where you are financially each month.

2. Is there a penalty if you pay the mortgage off early, or pay off a lump sum? It's best to find a mortgage that allows you to do this without incurring a fine.

3. Will the mortgage allow you to take a break – that is, stop paying for six months if you're made redundant or decide to go travelling?

4. Can you get a cash lump sum at the beginning of the mortgage to help you buy furniture, cover legal costs, and so on?

5. Are you borrowing too much? Are you leaving yourself vulnerable to changing interest rates, and therefore the risk of losing your home?

As soon as you've found an offer that suits you, ask for an Approval in Principle letter from the lender. This will come in handy to convince the estate agent and the vendor that you are a genuine purchaser and ready to move quickly. To get this you will need to provide evidence of your income and commitments, bank statements and proof of identity.

NB As soon as you start looking to buy a property, spend some time learning what terms such as 'gazumping' mean (the seller abandons your offer for a higher bid at a dishonourably late stage), as well as market and mortgage rate predictions for the next year.

The perfect legal brain

There isn't really such a thing as the perfect legal brain, but finding a great solicitor or lawyer who really keeps on top of your move and fights your corner is terribly important and a good investment. Ask friends and family to recommend one if you can.

The solicitor has to do a number of fiddly tasks for you: obtain the deeds, research the property's legal boundaries, prepare a list of fixtures, fittings and contents, advise you on the draft contract to sell from the vendor's solicitor, carry out a search on local planning, and agree a date for completion that suits you and the vendor – as well as helping to get you there with as little stress and fighting as possible.

Only you know how much money you have and how much you can afford to go up to, but make an offer and think rationally if you get into a bidding war. And don't let the searching stop there; keep researching and looking around the area to see if you're still getting the best deal. Be prepared: with this many legal and financial dramas and details, things can go wrong, but try not to be disheartened. Dream houses are like good men: there are plenty more fish in the sea!

JILL, 36

❝ My husband and I really pushed ourselves when we bought our house to borrow as little in the form of a mortgage as possible, and over a short period of ten years. We put every penny we had into the deposit and really didn't have much of a life for a good few years, as our high payments meant that we didn't have lots of disposable income. But we were so happy being in our home that it didn't matter! And now the property has quadrupled in value, and we have the money to redecorate the place, and it's been the location of our best dinners and parties ever. ❞

Packing up your home perfectly

◆ Start collecting boxes and old newspapers as soon as you know you are moving.

◆ Call in the cavalry. Get your partner to do his fair share, and if you have kids make them responsible for sorting through unwanted toys they don't want to take to the new house.

◆ Treat moving as a good excuse to do a thorough spring clean. If you haven't used something for over a year, you probably never will. Dump it.

◆ Talk to your local council or borough about coming to the house a few days before you move to pick up big items of rubbish and old furniture to save you a trip to the dump.

◆ Buy lots of masking tape and thick black marker pens. Write a mini inventory of contents on each box, and the room in which it belongs clearly on the top and side.

◆ Packing always takes longer than you think. Keep the four weekends before the move free and set yourself a timetable of rooms to be finished by a certain point.

◆ Keep all important documents together and keep those with you during the move (or leave them at a safe house like your mum's).

Secrets of Success

◆ At the beginning of a new year, open your chequebook and write in the new year in the date line of your next 25 cheques. We all get this wrong for the first few months and that means ripping them up and starting again. This will save time – and cheques!

◆ Always open your post and check what's inside. Even if it's just a boring bank statement, open, read, chuck the rubbish and file just the important bits.

◆ You know who are the cheapest financial advisors of all? Your friends and family – they've been there, done it and more than anyone else in the world, have your best interests at heart. If they offer to lend you money for a deposit or to get you out of debt, accept graciously (don't be too proud!) and pay them back asap – with a little something extra to say thanks (not cash, a well-planned gift!).

◆ If you're saving, entertain more at home than going to fancy restaurants – but organise your mates to help out! You can supply the space, the party games and the music; other people can bring the rest. This is a cheap way to socialise.

◆ If your saving is limiting your wild partying for a few months, investigate free things in the local community or take the free time (and lack of alcohol consumption) to get organised on a health kick. Running is free, and swimming at your local pool is cheap!

◆ When organising your budgets – be it weekly, monthly or yearly – always overestimate, don't underestimate. If things turn out well, you can treat yourself at the end of the year, which will be more fun than wondering where your money has gone.

◆ If you can afford it, hiring professional packers when you move is a desirable luxury. They're insured against breakages and literally take all the weight of moving off your shoulders. They can be pricey, however, so get a few quotes, compare prices and try to strike up a deal.

Chapter Five

Office order

SADLY, MY DARLING GIRLS, we seem to spend more time in the office these days than with our loved ones. Although a well-organised modern girl should trim every corner and make every second count – so that she can run free at a reasonable hour each night – problems and dramas do occur that keep us chained to our desks. That's why we need a proper code of behaviour and an efficient manner in our place of work more than anywhere else. Work is bad enough without office politics and fighting colleagues.

Being punctual, polite and fluster-free

There are basic levels of etiquette that need to be strictly enforced at all times in the workplace:

- Arrive at a meeting on time (even early, to get yourself sorted and pick the best seat – the one opposite your boss if you want to impress, next to your boss if you want to show support, or down the bank of chairs on the right if you want to hide). If you're going to be late, call or email ahead. It will save you that mortifying 'sorry' entrance when everything is in full swing.

- Keep a notepad and a (working) pen with you at all times.

- Always say good morning or good afternoon, and offer a firm handshake and a look in the eye when meeting your colleagues or clients for the first time in the day.

- Carry business cards with you – it will save you time writing down your contact details.

- Ten minutes before a meeting, look through your files and diary, and check that you are prepared. If you're not, quickly ask a friendly colleague for the lowdown – and repay the favour when he or she needs help. Do not make asking for help a regular occurrence, though, as people will think you are lazy or stupid and word will filter upwards.

◆ Never, ever go to work in the same shirt you wore the day before. And never, ever go into the office with a stain or tear in anything.

◆ Even if minutes are not being prepared officially after a meeting, take five minutes to make a note to yourself about what was discussed and the aims for the future.

◆ In a meeting, if any task is given to you, make a note of all the details immediately – you will forget!

◆ Remember to turn your phone off in a meeting – unless you are expecting a very urgent call, in which case explain that it might ring, and apologise.

◆ Even if there are big trays of muffins displayed in the middle of the table, don't make it your personal mission to munch your way through all of them. Look at what other people are taking and don't be a piggy – grab a sandwich afterwards. The main purpose of this time is to strategise and coordinate, not to embarrass yourself at the buffet.

◆ If someone takes time to come and see you, debrief you or help you generally, always say thank you and follow up with a 'much appreciated' email.

Work is incredibly important, and you should treat every minute there as a chance to prove you are intelligent, motivated and have a bright future. But other aspects of your life are just as, if not more, important. Make every minute in the office count, and then try to forget about it when you leave. If you don't, you'll soon become disheartened and resentful, and everything will suffer.

ANNA, 28

❝ Work was taking over my life so much I set a rule: I could worry about it until I'd served up dinner, then I'd switch off and enjoy my family time. It doesn't always work. But at least I try! ❞

How to communicate effectively

We spend more of the time in the office talking or writing to others than working on projects. We need to, of course, because batting away other people's issues and instilling them with faith are must-dos – but we can waste time (ours and theirs) spending too long communicating.

Phone tips to save time

◆ Hold your phone with whichever hand you don't write with; this will free you up to write notes at the same time.

◆ If you're in the flow and need to concentrate, let the phone go to voicemail. We're trained like Pavlov's dogs to answer every time the phone rings, but we shouldn't feel compelled to if we can't be interrupted. Make sure you have a clear answering-machine message, asking for all details, and giving a time within which you will return the call (24 hours is fine).

◆ Likewise, leaving messages rather than talking directly to someone can be an efficient and time-saving tool. Leave a message saying exactly what you need and by when, with clear instructions on how to reach you.

♦ If leaving a message with another person, ask them to repeat it back to you so that all the details are correct – and perhaps even ask if they can help you. It might be quicker than waiting for your contact to call you back.

♦ Modern phones have many different functions, which you should use to be more effective. Ask how to use 'call forwarding', 'conference calling', 'do not disturb' and the answering machine as soon as you get a new phone.

Avoid telephone tag

Trying to catch telephone-shy people is a total waste of time and an organised girl's worst nightmare! Some people are terrible at returning calls, or simply don't review their voice messages. If this is happening to you, try another form of communication – email or fax, or if they're in the same building, get off your ass and go to see them. Or try teasing them into calling you back. Don't give all the details, and cheekily make your reason for calling sound more interesting than it really is. You can also try being specific: call me by 3.00 p.m. or we're going to lose this deal. That should do it. And don't worry about being forceful. If, after you have left two messages you have still had no reply, they are officially being rude!

Email tips to save time

1. Don't feel the need to print out every email – just important attachments and proposals. You might feel nervous leaving everything on a computer, but there is no need to print. Just immediately copy important dates and names into your diary or notepad.

2. Ease your email load! Get off random email lists, explain to friends that you don't want generic emails, and ask your company IT department to protect you from spam. If you're being cc-ed on emails unnecessarily, ask for it to stop. Ask friends to email you on a private account.

3. Every email seems urgent – it pops up menacingly and sometimes even bleeps on arrival! But don't get sucked into checking messages every minute. Turn off the 'new email alarm' if you can. Read important emails when they come in, then remind yourself to go back to them by marking them 'unopened'.

4. If an email requires just a quick yes, no or accepted answer – don't procrastinate. Email users aren't expecting an essay. Just reply immediately, jot down details and delete it. Like ticking off to-do lists, deleting emails feels good!

5. Set up folders within your email system as an easy and quick-to-use storage facility. Name them in capitals by name of project, or the person's name, or by urgency so that they are easy to see. This will help you look back and find the correct message quickly, rather than trawling though your whole inbox. Also, store important messages you have sent in a separate folder.

NB Don't get sucked into long discussions on the phone or get guilt-tripped into sending long and thoughtful emails when you're at work. Keep things polite and brief. If you need to get your mum off the office phone, just say so, and promise to call her at the weekend. If, on the other hand, it's a client or colleague on the phone but they've meandered into random ramblings, pretend you have a meeting, or that someone has just walked into your office – and that if they haven't covered everything now, could they send an email.

How to make the most of your day

Do you ever get into your office full of purpose, then start surfing the web, and chatting to the girl next door, and then head out for coffee ... and before you know it you've wasted a day and you either have to stay late to catch up, or you go home but feel guilty and dread the next day? Well, this workplace procrastination can and should be avoided – it doesn't help anyone, and with a little less waffle, you'll be getting home in time for *Desperate Housewives*.

Be prime-time focused: we all have a time of the day, or month, when we feel more energised and efficient. It could be Mondays, or the week after your period, or Wednesday mornings after you've been to the gym. Use this time to power through your most important and difficult tasks. Arrange meetings, appointments and lunches around other times.

Don't feel like you always have to have an open door. Even if you're not in your own office and can't physically shut yourself away, mentally make a 60-minute appointment with yourself. Don't allow distractions – so, no checking emails or making calls, or answering colleagues' questions. Stay focused on your most desperate tasks of the day and clear your back catalogue of work. Don't answer the phone when it rings during this time (unless your boss's name flashes up), just make sure you have a good answering-machine message and that there's room to take new messages.

Avoid impromptu meetings. All too often I'm busy doing

something, when someone comes in to ask something, I get a few people in for their opinion and before you know it, we're in a fully fledged meeting, where everyone is going off on tangents. If people do this, be upfront and say you're busy right now, but set time aside to meet later.

Think about when to time important meetings. Monday meetings can become a chore and something to dread over the weekend. Grab people on a Thursday when the weekend is in sight and they've had a few days to mull over new concepts in the office. Plan your next day's work the day before, and, if you are the boss, give out everyone's work the afternoon before. This will give them time to plan their day and workflow. Plus, it will give them time to muse over what needs to be done on their commute home and back the next day.

Make appointments back to back to limit start and stop times, or to minimise breaking your flow when you've got something serious going on. This will also help you to finish each appointment on time. You should be adding deadlines and end points to all meetings anyhow, but knowing you have another meeting to get to helps. And don't schedule 15-minute respites in between meetings – if you need to run to the loo, you can do that while your new meeting buddies are getting settled in their seats.

Always aim to finish a project a few days before it's official 'time up' moment. If it's due on Friday, aim to have it in by Wednesday to allow time for technical issues, emergencies and feedback.

If you have a few big jobs on, set a schedule – and put the bigger, more urgent and more difficult tasks at the beginning of your timeline. Somehow, even for the most organised girl, time gets eaten up and disappears towards the end of the week. And always allow yourself more time than you think you'll need – if you finish early, consider it a bonus.

Don't feel bad about saying no. If you've got a lot on your plate, politely excuse yourself from company away days, meetings or lunches. Your commitment is to reaching your professional goals. Say yes to such appointments when you've got some time to play with.

Keep your work calendar or diary with you at all times. It saves time when you can't remember where you have to be at a certain time. If you're serious about getting organised, write down tasks, appointments and deadlines in your diary in pen. Writing them in pencil screams, 'I can change anything if I want to.' No – get discipline from ink!

NB Passers-by and parasites! Gosh, everyone wants a bit of you! If people are hanging around your desk and interrupting your flow with questions, ask how long they will take, and don't feel bad asking them to come back if need be. Also ask if this is really your problem to solve or can someone else help. If it's clear that this person does need you urgently, ask them to hold on for one second while you quickly note where you are and what thoughts you'd just had, before you forget.

Delegation!

Some people don't like to delegate. They're either control freaks or nervous wrecks, worried that some young up-and-comer will steal their glory! But, you know what, laydeez? Let it go! Use the talented and motivated people around you to help you become a good manager and to get out of the office on time. Sure, if there's nothing else on, do all your work yourself, but if you're pushed for time, write a to-do list and take charge of the things that will really benefit from your skill set. Then be realistic about passing other tasks out to your junior team, or asking a peer if they don't mind. But remember three things when delegating: debrief the person fully and clearly, and give them all the relevant information; set a deadline and check in regularly without being overbearing; and give them credit where credit is due – that way they won't mind helping you again!

SHIRLEY, 45

❝There is definitely a difference between your own time management and paid-employment time management. The former is always harder to handle – I don't know why, but it is! You can be the most efficient person in the company, but when it comes to getting children to parties or waxing your legs, the day will fall apart and appointments overlap, so you're late and stressed! But if you can tell good white lies you're OK for a while. Embarrassingly, though, when I last went to the dentist and was given my notes to take upstairs, I sneaked a quick look and was mortified to see 'always late'. I now run my home life efficiently, like I do my office! ❞

Office organisational no-nos!

These mistakes suck the life out of the organised girl. Make sure you don't commit them!

The first problem is trying to work from a disorganised, messy area. A recent study showed that people who have an untidy workstation spend on average one-and-a-half hours more per day looking for things and getting sidetracked than the person with a neat desk. Don't spend your day in the office clueless as to what you need to prioritise. Set yourself a plan and a deadline – don't just answer the needs of who-ever shouts (or moans) the loudest. Stick to your guns.

Some of your colleagues may think they deserve a medal for working through their lunch break, but don't make mar-tyrs of them just yet. After three hours of working, our attention fades and creative thoughts can slow down. Studies show that escaping for half an hour can reawaken us, recharge our batteries and help to get a new perspective on things.

Likewise, some people feel all worthy if they stay late into the evening. So should you feel bad if you're always one of the first to leave? No way – if you've got everything done or something can wait until tomorrow, get out of there. As a manager of 45 staff, I'm always suspicious if members of my team need to be in the office hours later than everyone else. Is their role too big for them? Do they spend too much time on the Internet during the day? Most bosses will be the same as me, so don't get trapped into a competitive game of 'I'm in the office last every night' – you're not impressing anyone.

And lastly, don't let lack of sleep jeopardise your work-ing day. People who suffer from a lack of sleep are not as progressive and organised in their work as their more rested colleagues. A good night's rest speeds you up and makes you more alert. If you're going to bed but still not feeling refreshed in the morning, look at the quality of your sleep. Is there too much light in the room, are you dehydrated, or are you working-out, eating or drinking coffee too late? Sort out your environment, because sleep is priceless.

The perfectly organised desk

Ah, the organised girl's haven! All else in the office might be mental, but a well-planned desk is her refuge. Think about the following to achieve office organisational heaven:

◆ Make sure you have plenty of drawers near your desk, and have stationery you use often in the handiest spot.

◆ Keep your desk tidy. Clear it every night before you leave, it'll help you the next day.

◆ Store all your permanent things on one side – your phone, your printer, your computer, your stapler, and so on – leaving the other side free for changing needs and products, and to allow you to spread out your work.

◆ If you can, set up your desk so that you're not sitting facing the door. Face a window to keep you alert, because if you face the door you'll be distracted by every waif and stray who wanders past.

◆ L- and U-shaped desks are the best for offering room to manoeuvre and surface space.

◆ Don't go overboard on the personal knick-knacks. One photo and one beauty product should do it. I got to the point once where I had three bottles of perfume, countless lip balms, a plant, a jar of Marmite and a mirror. It drove me insane and my desk always looked a mess. Shoving all that rubbish in my drawer gave me peace of mind, and didn't take any longer to grab.

◆ But remember: a tidy desk is different for everyone. Some people demand that nothing is seen, and even put their keypad in the drawer at the end of a day. Others like pens and papers neatly stacked to one side. Choose your own style.

◆ Use hanging folders, wire baskets, stacking trays and the bin to keep your desk clear of paperwork. Read everything and file it or bin it. Don't think, 'I'll read it again and deal with it later.'

♦ Don't waste your space by hoarding envelopes and staples. Keep what you need. The stationery cupboard won't run out. Apply the three-quarters rule: when you've gone through three-quarters of your stuff, you need to get more.

SABRINA, 30

❝ Our company puts on lots of large-scale events and it is really important that we pull together as a team and are super-organised on the day. As much as possible I will try to give our jobs to people according to what they enjoy doing, or want to learn more about. This way you are most likely to get the best out of everyone. If there is a rubbish job to do I make sure we all take a turn so that each one of us only has to do it for a short time. ❞

Working from home

This is a dream for many women – me included. The idea of getting up at a time that suits you, not struggling through bad weather and train delays, and getting to stop at lunchtime to meet a friend for an hour or two sounds blissful. But stop this dream from turning into a nightmare by staying focused if you are working from home:

♦ Get dressed! And don't put the television on! Having a home office means working from home in a professional environment. Don't lie-in then lounge around in your pyjamas making tea. You're not off sick, this is your new life plan, and to make it work you need to put the hours in.

◆ Plan your hours. You'll be saving on commuting and office politics time, but you still need to put a full day in. Work on your body clock – if you're an early riser, for example, you could start at 8.00 a.m. and be finished by 2.00 p.m.!

◆ Create a home office, somewhere away from interruptions with a safe place for all documents and business equipment. Don't go in there when you are not working. Keep it a professional space. If you haven't got a separate room, make a separate area – but never in the bedroom! It's a stress-grower and passion-killer!

◆ Keep all business costs noted and invoices saved. This will make claiming tax much easier.

◆ Don't necessarily announce to the world that you're now working from home – this will encourage the world and his neighbour 'to pop by, as you're home'. And don't get sucked into chats with the milkman or postman.

Office moral dilemmas answered

Q *I'd rather focus my energy on my work in the office. Do I have to socialise with colleagues?*

A Well, it depends who is asking, if it's your boss or your boss's boss, sadly you have to go unless you have a cast-iron reason not to. Suck it up and make the most of it by impressing everyone around you, as well as getting tips and guidance for your own career. If it's your peers who are asking, do enough not to appear a party pooper – but not so much that they think you don't have any friends! If they're your juniors, take them out or attend a gathering and have fun – but don't get drunk and talk badly about people senior to them.

Q *I'm scared to ask for a pay rise – how can I motivate myself?*

A Don't compare yourself to anyone else and don't demand a raise because you need money (your boss doesn't care if you're stupid enough to max out your credit card!). Approach with a factual list of all your achievements, your gains for the company, and all the things you have done above and beyond the call of duty, and certainly over your job description, which your salary is based on. Don't give an ultimatum unless you are prepared to walk.

Q *How can I avoid a colleague I dislike or don't trust?*

A Organise your schedule to be away from this person. Don't attend optional events where he or she will be. But if you do bump into each other, be polite. And in the company of others, stay diplomatic. If he or she is that terrible, the boss will find out soon enough anyway. If asked a direct question about their value to the company, answer professionally and steer clear of personal remarks.

Secrets of Success

◆ Paper diary or PDA? Have both. I find physically writing things down helps me to remember stuff, but a PDA is handy, as it can do many things at many times.

◆ Don't worry if someone teases you for being an anal, organised freak at work – they're probably jealous, as they feel buried under a pile of half-done, un-filed work projects. A filing system, an up-to-date diary and a neat desk are the three biggest keys (or make that lifesavers) at work – and they help to get you out of the office on time.

◆ Organising your work life takes on a force of its own when you have children. I'm not qualified to say anything (because I don't have any) except: think what's important in the long term – your children and being with them, or your boss's profits? Do what you can without being driven crazy, and talk about options with your human resources people when you tell them you're pregnant.

◆ Working from home with your partner or housemate will work only if you have separate areas, separate computers and separate phones, so organise this immediately.

◆ The higher up the ladder you go, the better you're going to have to get about organising. You'll have to manage up and manage down, and fit a thousand different requests and needs into your already packed schedules. Learn to prioritise, delegate and enjoy the career you've chosen – or get out!

Chapter Six

Me time: work vs play vs nothing

So, WHEN YOU'VE JUST about finished organising the office, your boss, your colleagues, your mother, the school run, your visit to the gym, and the laundry basket – phew – how about looking after yourself, and organising yourself some fun (even if that involves little more than a tub of Häagen Dazs and a Renée Zellweger movie)?

Can women have it all?

Well, I hope so; otherwise what are we fighting for? But what we can't expect is to have it all and feel happy all the time. We're super-brilliant but not super-human, and everyone has moments of feeling stressed, tired, emotional, undervalued, mad and lonely. What we can't have is 'it all' without any help – from your partner, your children, your family, your colleagues (and not just the ones down the career ladder from you, but the ones you look up to as well).

So, never feel bad about admitting you need help – and then asking for it! If you really feel you have bitten off more than you can chew (and who hasn't felt like that at some point?), sit down and take stock. Ask the opinions of people you trust and who have been there themselves. Sit down with a blank piece of paper and write down what is troubling you and what needs to be changed. Delaying matters won't help anything or anyone – and rational decisions are harder to make after a run of sleepless nights. Organise your internal chaos, don't deny it.

How to handle impostor syndrome

I suffer from this, do you? The feeling that you've suddenly landed in the big boys' world and you don't know how. You dismiss your success as luck and feel unworthy of praise – or even a pay rise. But luck has very little to do with it. Rearrange your brain: you've got where you are through hard work, intelligence, courage and commitment – don't let anyone tell you otherwise.

Organising balance

Sometimes, when your life is so busy and overwhelming, it's best to take a step back and look at where you've become so unbalanced. If you're not enthusiastic about a certain area in your life and your heart's not in it, it could be because you're working at it to make other people happy rather than yourself. Here are ten ways to stop work taking over your life, or your spare time undermining your professional pizzazz. Really, how can you be happy?

1. Keep a time diary – even if it's just for a few weeks. This will help you focus on exactly what you are doing with your day, and whether you are spending too much time in the office or taking too many long, boozy lunch hours.

2. Plan your daily, weekly, monthly and yearly ambitions. Set yourself a standard and a timeline – and keep to it. Imagine the life you want in five years' time and get on the path that takes you there asap.

3. Check in with yourself on a regular basis to make sure you are on the right track and not being forced into a lifestyle corner. Decide what is important to you.

4. Remember that looking after your own personal needs will give you the enthusiasm and energy to take on the more gruelling things in life.

5. Take action to turn dreams into reality. Ask yourself questions all the time: how can I get more energy? Who is there for me? What are my beliefs? What habits and routines should I start to get more out of my day?

6. Small things can make a big difference. Don't put off small tasks, as they will soon mount into huge problems. And remember that big tasks seem smaller when tackled on time, in the right order.

7. Don't just plan for the year ahead with new year's resolutions – looking back can be even more useful. Do an end-of-year audit to re-evaluate your life; ask yourself what you have most enjoyed last year. What have you learned? What are you proud of? What has disappointed you?

8. It's normal to feel a 'wobble' when your life is unbalanced; go with it and question what you really want and need before pushing any fears to the back of your mind.

9. Look at your roles as daughter, mother, friend, partner, boss, colleague, team player, and so on – and think about what your favourite roles are. Spend 80 per cent of your time and energy on the important ones.

10. Write down and schedule time for yourself. Don't let anyone feel that this means you are selfish or lazy. If you don't actually make a plan for it, the chances are that 'me time' will be the first thing to disappear when things get tough, and it shouldn't be that way.

> **SHIRLEY,** 50
>
> ❝Sometimes life can get of top of you and you need to organise your life quickly and easily to get your sanity back. So, occasionally I file my paperwork in the shredder, serve dinners pre-packed from Marks & Spencer and don't mind being the bossy bitch at work, if it means getting things done. Quite frankly, I take shortcuts – and it feels good. ❞

Juggling work and children

My friends with children rely heavily on caring partners and giving parents, plus qualified childcare specialists. The following things also help:

◆ Hire people to clean and do your laundry if it allows more quality time with the kids, and get the kids helping with chores, too, so you're not running around for them when you are home. A ten-year-old can put clothes away and make a bed.

◆ Try to work as close to home as possible, even at home if that's realistic. You don't want to commit to a five-hour shift but then spend three hours on the road commuting.

◆ If you don't ask, you don't get. If you want to work shorter hours or fewer days, go to your boss or the human resources manager.

◆ Get up half an hour earlier to complete household chores before the kids get up.

◆ Don't waste time feeling guilty; if you love working, that's fine. Just make sure when you are with your children, you have time to do things with them, chat and enjoy time together.

> **NB if you're working from home,** set some rules. Give yourself a space that is yours and that the family can't get into. Have a secure phone line installed so that the kids can't interrupt your business. Don't become isolated – find time to keep up with your colleagues. Also, invest in on-line courses and web-chat communities. Be selfish and say no if work falls outside your remit. Don't treat working from home like a chance to lie around in your pyjamas watching daytime television. Get up at a decent time, get washed, get dressed and get yourself psychologically ready to give it your all (even if you're giving it at your kitchen table!).

How much time should be spent on you?

Spend as much time on yourself as you need, without everything around you falling apart. Some people get their self-fulfilment and pleasure from constantly making sacrifices for others, financially and emotionally. If you're not such an Angelina Jolie, don't worry. Take the phone off the hook, ignore your friends' pleas for a girls' night out and don't feel you have to go to every work event. Clear your diary and take a deep breath.

We've been kind of sped-up to a mad degree. Modern life dictates we rush around and shouldn't be enjoying slow, easy things like country walks or listening to the radio while sewing, and so on. But a group of my friends are rebelling and calming down their lives – not burning the candle at both ends, panicking if they miss the gym, or competing with the neighbours over the garden fence. They are cutting down friendship groups to the nearest and nearest, not planning huge parties or holidays, and rediscovering why they love their families and partner. And you know what? They look younger, seem calmer and have a contentedness I admire – and some day wish to possess.

SHANIA, 25

❛My tried-and-true tip for being organised is to put everything in the same place. I have a beautiful silver bowl that makes me smile every time I look at it, and in there I place all my smaller items like keys, wallet, spare change, passport, etc. I now do this without thinking, and I never lose anything. The time it saves allows me to spend longer straightening my hair in the morning!❜

Have we got there yet?

Part of the reason for speed and stress is this hideous need to make things bigger and better and brighter. Modern girls very rarely stop for a time and look back at what they've achieved; they're too busy looking ahead and worrying that their peers are swallowing them up. But do stop. Be proud of what you've done. Ten years ago, I bet you weren't so financially stable, and I imagine your hair was shocking! Organise enough time into your life to stop and congratulate yourself.

When work and free time collide, here's how to use your lunch breaks and commute time wisely. Your boss doesn't pay you while you're sitting on the bus on your way into the office, or for the extra hour you sit at your desk picking up other people's mistakes, so reclaim this time when you can.

Lunch breaks

◆ Join the work gym or ask about corporate memberships to nearby places. Thirty minutes of cardio is easily doable in an hour's lunch break!

◆ Get a book club started with your friends in the office, and meet once a week in a local coffee shop.

◆ Hit the shops, even if you're skint – window-shopping is a great relaxant.

◆ Force yourself to buy a sandwich a mile away, and take a pleasant stroll.

◆ Bring in your lunch then head to the canteen with your mobile to catch up with family and friends.

◆ Spend the hour doing your weekly food shop on the Internet.

◆ Take time to do personal chores: call your doctor, schedule a hair appointment, book a holiday, and write some birthday or staying-in-touch cards.

◆ Get all your bitching and office politics off your chest with a trusted colleague over a glass of wine down the road.

Commute time

◆ Use the time to do your make-up, either for the office, or for a night out after a day at work.

◆ Learn some stomach-tightening and butt-clenching exercises that are invisible to the naked eye to help you tone while travelling.

◆ In the morning, read at least one newspaper so that you're abreast of the world's dramas and funny stories.

◆ Escape with a good book – nothing passes the time quicker.

◆ Make sure you download at least one new album a month onto your iPod and really get to know it.

◆ Likewise, download podcasts of missed radio shows and talking books, and educate yourself easily.

◆ Take up a minimal-space hobby like knitting, sewing or crocheting.

◆ Write a diary or chapter plans for your first novel.

◆ Try to travel in or out of work with your partner, and promise to use that time only as 'work' time – at home it's 'us' time. But remember, whether in person or while on the phone, avoid using commuting time to have a really loud personal conversation. Remember: everyone else around you wants to chill out and escape into his or her own little world, too.

ANDREA, 31

❝ I actually organised my whole wedding on the train in and out of work every morning over a period of six months. I called everyone I needed to – including my maddening mother – between the hours of 9.00 a.m. and 10.00 a.m., and then on my way home from work I'd write notes and a wedding to-do list for the following morning. I didn't forget anything ... except the karaoke machine, which in hindsight was a good thing! ❞

Timetabling your free time

Sometimes it's necessary to organise doing absolutely nothing! My boyfriend and I actually make a commitment in our diaries to do nothing on Friday nights: our date night/ free romantic time. And sometimes you should do that, too. If you know you're tired on Monday after the weekend, pencil in a 'video and takeaway night'; every Wednesday, head for a swim alone. Be strong and keep these commitments. Don't sell them to others as floating commitments with yourself; treat them as if they're rock solid. That free time could be the difference between going mad – and not!

Squeezing in a hobby

Here are some easy tricks to keep you open and able to enjoy new talents and the things you love:

◆ Persuade a friend to join you; they'll keep your motivation high, and give you a sense of commitment.

◆ Keep all the kit you need for your hobby in your car (if you drive to and from work) or in your office, in case you're kept late at work and don't have time to go home first.

◆ Rather than joining a gym or college near home, find one near to the office. It'll be a chore packing your bag in the morning but you'll have fewer chances of missing it, or catching the 'I can't be bothered' bug after a dire commute.

◆ Don't have a hobby that you think will impress your boss, or make you look cool. Choose something that you will love – that will ensure you squeeze it in.

◆ If you can't see a new project fitting into your everyday life, take an intense course in a hobby. Go on a week-long yoga retreat or perhaps take a few weekends at an artist's commune to perfect your painting.

◆ Use your Saturdays. If the thought of squeezing in evening classes or sports after works stresses you out, look for things to do on a Saturday, and try to persuade your partner to join you, if that is your usual hang-out time.

◆ Eat dinner (or a snack at least) at the office, or while commuting, before you go to your class, gym or whatever. I've too often been put off making it to the swimming pool after work because I'm too hungry!

◆ Have two kinds of hobby: an action hobby, and a de-stress hobby. And keep one going at any point in your life. I have a personal trainer for when I'm feeling full of beans, and photography when I just need some quiet time.

◆ Reach for blue sky. Embrace fear. Never think that you won't be able to achieve something, and set yourself a challenge: sign up for next year's marathon, train to scuba dive in your local pool so that you can swim among the fishes on your next vacation, start writing poetry and submit it to local competitions.

♦ Pay up-front for a course – the dislike of losing money will keep you going.

♦ Choose the right time to start. Everyone likes to hibernate in the winter, so don't choose February to start long- distance running.

♦ Tell everyone you've started something, so you'll be embarrassed not to continue or improve!

HOW NOT TO LOSE FRIENDS AND ALIENATE PEOPLE

... even when you're busy at work!

1. Send a generic email every few days to your friends and family, with snippets of fresh info and a few good wishes. But don't just forward junk mail. Take one minute to do something personal.

2. Keep a stack of blank greetings cards in your desk drawer to send to a friend on any occasion.

3. Be upfront and honest. If you're tied to your desk and you can't make an arrangement for dinner, say so in advance – don't ever feel it's better to accept and then drop out at the last minute. You'll feel guilty and they'll have to rearrange things. And after only a few times of doing it, everyone will think you're a flake!

4. Commit time to people in the future: a holiday, or a decadent new year's eve bash.

5. Explain how tough life is for you at the moment, but promise them champagne when the deal or promotion comes through.

6. Ask for help. People like to feel needed. Get your friends to recommend someone, or help you at the weekend with something. This isn't a sign of weakness; this is a sign that you trust them.

7. Don't be rude – always return a phone message, even if it's a clipped 30 seconds on your way to the loo!

8. Now is the time to lose the hangers-on and donate what time you do have to the people you will want in your life in ten years' time.

9. Get a cleaner and let your workout routine suffer a bit. If it means spending more time making yourself happy, these are small sacrifices.

10. Recognise when the job is destroying your social life, friendships and peace of mind. When is enough, enough? Is your boss taking the mickey? Are you really happy living behind a desk covered in paper? And do the company appreciate your efforts anyway? Keep analysing!

Negativity? No way!

The quickest way, I've found, to save time – and make more time for really important people and places – is to cut out the negative things from my life. Not only do you tend to spend a lot of mental energy justifying the no good, the bad and the ugly, but they eat up your hours, too!

We all have friends who we've known for years (or even some newish ones who we've met at work and bonded with too quickly), or even relatives who you keep around you because they're 'blood' – but who make you feel like shite. They put you down, don't ask you any questions, or sniff at your accomplishments and you leave after a few hours feeling a bit down and depressed. And you wonder why. It's because they're sucking the life out of you. They're jealous or bitter and not good to be around. So fade these people out politely but firmly by not returning calls, only sending curt email responses, and by gently refusing invitations. Spend this saved time (and emotional sanity) on your true friends and supporters. I was forced to do this when I moved from London to New York, because when I'd return for a weekend I had limited time to spend with people, and it has worked a treat. My relationships with the people I adore have improved and I don't feel 'guilt-tripped' into spending time with people who don't wish me well.

Horrid habits

Everyone has bad habits. Mine is picking my split ends. I literally go into a trance, hypnotised by how bleaching my hair for five years has turned my 'do' into a straw-like mess. But I've forced myself to stop. Instead, I make sure I get a haircut every eight weeks and use a deep-conditioning treatment. If you have any time-wasting bad habits, just say now, 'I'm going to stop them!' I stopped by thinking I could have an extra 15 minutes in bed reading if I halted this disgusting habit. Think of the time you'd save if you stopped smoking/bitching/picking your spots/getting drunk and therefore hung-over, and so on.

Office politics

Everyone gets sucked into the 'he said/she said/the boss said' wars at some point, but try to keep your nose clean and avoid water-cooler negativity, and you'll be amazed at how much quicker you get out of the door each day. If a colleague comes to you with a genuine problem, try to solve it as fairly and calmly as possible, then let that be it. Don't then spend the next hour gossiping about the drama to your friend in accounts.

Bad experiences

We can all dwell on our past too much. Nasty boyfriends, rude bosses, the time we got drunk in Rio, the time we put on two stone when we'd been dumped. This emotional procrastinating can take up a lot of time. Analyse and torment yourself with your past for one intense period, then move on.

Secrets of Success

◆ Sometimes it's good to be selfish! Yes, I know we're not supposed to be self-centred but it sure feels good. If you don't fancy a drink with your colleagues or you don't have time to spend your Saturday searching for a 'pulling' outfit with your mate, politely and firmly say no – and do what you want to do (even if it's just staying in bed with a few magazines all day!).

◆ Don't submit yourself to morning madness. Spend a few minutes when you all get in at night planning what you need the next morning – be it money, a signed letter or a book. This will stop the desperate searching in the morning.

◆ Perform a life inventory: make a list of everything that's important and everything you can live without. Work out your own scheme of valuing which areas have more weight and therefore deserve more time.

◆ Organising free time sounds like a contradiction in terms but you do have to put yourself first sometimes, and that will mean scheduling an appointment for something you personally need as seriously as you would an appointment with your bank manager.

◆ Save time organising your home life by keeping a shelf or storage closet near to the front door where all coats, umbrellas, shoes and bags belong.

◆ Life is too short to be constantly thinking about others. What do you want to do? What are you scared you will regret not having done when you're old?

◆ If a friend is really dragging you down and not taking the hint, meet up for a drink and tell them that you feel you've outgrown each other and neither of you is gaining anything from your friendship. Call it a day – and make it clear you're not joking. The same goes for ex-boyfriends.

Chapter Seven

Making the most of weekends

PURE BLISS! WEEKENDS ARE what us busy working folk live for: the opportunity to escape the nine-to-five routine (or more realistically the nine-to-seven) and decide how we want to spend our time, in our own way and at our own pace.

Thank God it's ...

Friday: the day the weekend truly starts! Try to keep big, dull tasks to a Thursday evening to keep Friday night clear (I always get the cleaner to come in on a Friday morning so that the flat is clean for the weekend, and do all my laundry and bank trips, etc., on a Thursday).

If you're going out straight from work on a Friday, it's worth having a grooming night in on Thursday. Wash your hair, plan your outfit and put extra make-up, and so on, in your handbag – you might forget it in the morning rush. Start your weekend fun early by planning an interesting lunch out, away from your desk, on a Friday. Escape with a fun bunch of girls from the office, or treat an interesting client to an all-expenses-paid feast.

If you get a spare few minutes on the way in to work, or on the way out, complete weekend chores that can be done on the phone: book a flight, order a book, check in with your siblings, organise your Saturday-night plans, for example.

If it's getting towards the end of the year and you still have a few days of holiday to take, think about taking Fridays (or Mondays) to extend your weekend. It's amazing what you can get done in one day when everyone else is at work – the shops, banks and post office are half-empty, so errands will take you half the time. Treat yourself to a manicure or pedicure, or a solo trip to the cinema to unwind for the weekend.

Lie-ins, love-ins and all that jazz

Most of us associate having a lazy morning in bed – sleeping, eating, reading, watching telly or getting it on with your partner – as one of life's greatest luxuries, worth more in the grand scheme of things than a massage once a month or a box of chocolates. All week we crave the alarm to stop and for us to be able to hide under the duvet for an extra few hours – then, on Saturday, it happens! So how can you make the most of these mornings?

1. Keep water by the bed so that you don't have to escape a snuggle in a moment of dehydration.

2. Turn off your alarm the night before! Don't let it ruin your blissful calm – an alarm bell will instantly put you back into the stressful situation of a Monday morning.

3. Invest in some decent curtains or blinds. Don't suffer with blinding early light for months; get it sorted as soon as you move into a new place. Your lie-ins will be wasted if you're not really getting any quality shut-eye!

4. If your easy mornings are about more than just catching up the week's sleep, prepare your blissful experience in advance. I know how tired you feel leaving work on Friday, but just gather an extra 30 minutes' worth of energy to make your way to the nearest supermarket. Pick up your favourite magazines, a TV guide and your favourite food – plus water, orange juice and milk – and you're sorted. You can hibernate all day if need be (something I totally recommend on a miserable day in February when you have no plans).

5. Turn off your mobile and take your phone off the hook. There's no point planning a lie-in if your mother calls you at 9.00 a.m. for chitchat.

The hangover

Eurgh – delirium tremens, sore throat, spinning head, delicate stomach, dead-cat dry mouth and a general malaise that makes you promise never to drink again – the morning joys of too much the night before! If you had any plans, they'll go out of the window. If you wanted to hit the gym, it won't happen. If you were going to clean your flat, fuggedibatit! Unless you are organised to a Stalin-regime-like level, you're buggered.

SARAH, 32

❝After work last summer, I hit the pub near work with my colleagues for a few post-office, de-stressing Pimm's with my colleagues. A glass turned to a jug, which turned to an endless fountain of the fruity beverage. I crawled into bed after a seven-hour drinking session at midnight. Which doesn't sound bad, except my cousin was getting married the next day and on the drive across London to the church, my dad had to pull over to let me vomit. I spent the day sipping water, unable to dance – and I looked positively green in all the photos. Delightful. ❞

I am useless with hangovers. A feeling that used to last for a few hours has extended into whole weekends (because some degree of sensibleness now keeps my extreme drinking to Friday nights) – and that means nothing gets done. So I've learned to control the amount of wastage in a few ways:

◆ It's boring, but drinking a glass of water between alcoholic drinks really does limit the damage.

◆ As does eating a hearty meal before a session, or even soaking it up with a kebab at the end of the night.

◆ Before going to bed perform a foolproof ritual: take two paracetamol washed down with a pint of water and a glass of orange juice, then head to the bathroom and take off all your make-up, moisturise your face and clean your teeth.

◆ It may be difficult to carry your arse into the shower, but if you can, the sensation of feeling clean and refreshed will be totally worth it – especially if you wash your hair free of grime and smoke.

◆ If you've got a truly busy, must-do day the next day – don't drink. If you can't go out and not drink, then don't go out. It's as simple as that. Everyone deserves a few duvet days, but don't get so hungover you miss something really important.

◆ If you are feeling like a ridiculous loser, avoid organised paragons of virtue like the plague. They will make you feel much, much worse – and could turn you to drink for good.

NB Don't allow the bitterness and regret of wasting a whole day in a drunken mess destroy your brain and will to live. I have literally been so pissed off at not having completed my list of chores because of my own stupidity that I've sat and cried, feeling like a failure. It's not worth it. Make yourself go to the gym for an extra session on the Monday, or keep the next weekend free for missed tasks.

Who to avoid at the weekend

Well, your boss is the most important one – and spending as little time as possible with anyone who reminds you of the pressures of your working week is highly recommended. Don't give over your whole weekend to the demands of your family. Mums can be persuasive, and you can feel required to help your dad paint the lounge – but stop, remember it's your downtime, too. Don't promise these people time and then let them down. Organise your diary clearly from the start.

And, in general, life is too short (as are weekends) to spend with people you don't like. If your partner has friends you're not keen on, limit time spent with them to a minimum – preferably on a less precious weeknight – and encourage him to go out with them and leave you to do your own thing.

What to avoid at the weekend

Well, a truly organised person would have completed the household chores and paperwork during the week, to leave these two free days for abseiling, potholing and fine dining. The rest of us will have to do a few boring things – but we shouldn't feel bad about that. I remember in my twenties, if someone asked me if I'd had a good weekend I'd feel very embarrassed if I didn't have much to say. Now I take absolute pleasure in saying, 'You know what, I can't remember. I did nothing, and it was lovely.' As long as you enjoy it, you don't have to avoid anything at the weekend.

ROBERTA, 35

❝ The best tip for effective time-management is to get up early – even at the weekend I'm up by 9.00 a.m. (a lie-in!). I leap out of bed and attack my list of things to do before I've fully woken up. At the weekend, you can get a lot done early because it's so quiet. Then, as time starts to dwindle, along with your list of chores, you get a smug sense of satisfaction knowing you're rushing around while everyone else is still snoozing. For an organised person like me, lying in bed knowing I have stuff to do will only increase my blood pressure. Normally, by midday, all is done and I stop for a delicious lunch and a much-deserved free afternoon. ❞

Instant relaxers

Don't waste time trying to unwind, instead:

◆ **Book a Friday-night/Saturday-morning spa session.** Massages and facials are super de-stressors.

◆ **Get up early and go hell-for-leather at the gym,** followed by a steam, sauna and Jacuzzi chill out.

◆ **Cut caffeine** – not just at weekends, but all week. Go for the herbal tea or Ovaltine option instead.

◆ **If something is upsetting or annoying you,** try to solve the problem by attacking it head-on before Friday, so that it can't ruin your weekend (it will when you have more time to think about it).

◆ **Don't over-plan.** I used to have the tendency to double-book myself at weekends, promising various friends I'd be able to meet them for lunch/shoppingtrips/coffee/dancing, and so on, then resenting them as I struggled with my diary or rushed around. I was so anxious that I didn't look forward to any of my plans. Now I'm more discerning: I've learned to say no.

◆ **Hippy pastimes can help you chill out.** Acupuncture, hypnotherapy and reiki healing are all fabulous at balancing inner peace with outer turmoil.

◆ **Make Friday night a TV and a takeaway night.** Plan it and look forward to it. My boyfriend and I have a 'cinema club' night – our little code for committing to an easy night of dinner and a movie every Friday. It's a simple way of making the transition from a busy week to a quiet weekend.

◆ **Invest in some candles and cool music,** take a long, hot soak, close your eyes and think about all the fun you're going to have over the next two days of free time.

◆ **Even if you're an anally retentive, type-A personality,** Reese Witherspoon type, it's good to relax sometimes. Call your family and oldest friends – they can tell you to relax or make fun of your antics, and you'll be forced to take a breath!

> **JACQUI, 25**
>
> 6 Learning to switch off is tough, especially with emails, mobile phones and Blackberrys constantly keeping you connected – whether you want to be or not. If I'm at a special dinner or party, or on holiday, I turn everything off. Believe it or not, things can wait until the morning. I also read a lot. Dipping into a good work of fiction provides the quickest escape route to another world. Get reading! 9

Weekend breaks

Ahhh, the mini-break – the stuff of Bridget Jones movies and new romances. There's no better way to make the most of a few days out of the office than taking off to a new environment.

If you're going overseas ...

◆ Spend a spare few minutes in the office, or on the Internet at home, investigating no-frills airlines and their short-distance special offers. A flight of three hours or less is more than doable at the weekend, if it's longer, try to take a day off.

◆ Work late each night and work through your lunch hours so that you can leave early on a Friday afternoon.

◆ Pack at home on Thursday and lug your suitcase into the office on Friday. It'll save time not having to go home again. Check in on-line if you can, to save an hour hanging around at the airport.

- If you can squeeze everything into a small carry-on bag, I highly recommend it. When you have precious few hours at the weekend, waiting at a baggage carousel for your luggage is tiresome.

If you're staying in the country ...

- Plan your train route and buy tickets in advance, or if you're driving, print out clear directions and fill your car up with petrol in advance.

- Arriving at your destination late? Tell the hotel beforehand, so that they can leave the fire on in your room, with a tasty late-night snack and a few drinks. You don't want to drive for miles to arrive hungry and thirsty at your destination, and find everything shut until morning.

- Ask the hotel or holiday centre to email you a list of events and things to do in advance, so that you can plan the best use of your limited amount of time.

- Pack little treats to make your trip super-enjoyable: his favourite chocolates, your favourite bubble bath, both of your favourite undies ...

- Make the most of your Sunday by planning a stop-off on the way back home – have afternoon tea in a quaint café, or have a late plate of roast beef and Yorkshire pudding in a country pub followed by a leisurely walk.

Monday-morning anxiety

I have wasted too many a good Sunday evening by worrying about Monday morning and the working week commencing – yet again! The best way to cure this, I've discovered, is by making interesting, non-drinking-related plans on a Sunday evening – be it a DVD at your best friend's house, going for a swim and steam with your boyfriend, or heading out to a fancy dinner with your family (it will be easier to get a reservation on a Sunday, remember).

And really, just focus on not ending your weekend after your roast dinner. Your company isn't paying for you to work for half of Sunday, so don't. Complete all urgent Monday tasks on Friday, and leave a to-do list on your desk for outstanding things for the following week. I find that as soon as you write something down, you worry about it less – your brain is free to enjoy other things. Don't stay out too late or drink too much vino on a Sunday – that'll kick your week off on the wrong foot, but don't feel you have to be in bed by 9.00 p.m. either – you won't sleep.

NB If you do find it hard to get to sleep on a Sunday night (so many of us do), a good rule to remember is to regulate your sleeping pattern all week long. Don't have extra-long lie-ins at the weekend, and then stay out until 4.00 a.m. on Fridays and Saturdays. If you do, what hope will you have of getting to sleep on Sunday night and waking refreshed on Monday? I've always found 'weekend afternoon naps' to be the most joyous thing, they feel very decadent – but don't tend to unsettle your sleeping routine as much.

Secrets of Success

◆ If you find yourself at a loose end at the weekend, don't feel like a boring loner – embrace it! Think about what you'd really like to do: if it's watching *Grease* and *Dirty Dancing* back to back in your pyjamas, now's the time to do it. And what could be better for your soul than that?

◆ If you know you'll relax more when your place is tidy, don't put it off – do it. Clear out those cupboards you've been meaning to, then reward yourself with a slice of your favourite cake and a few newspapers.

◆ If you have a significant other, the weekend really is your key time together. Don't organise your diary to a point that he's excluded – or will be miserable with your decisions.

◆ Ask friends for help if you've got a big weekend project on, like preparing to move house or decorating. Make it fun by treating them to a takeaway or get an easy buffet-and-booze lunch together. If some friends say no, don't resent them – who blames them?

◆ Weekends are precious – try to keep work trips and overtime to a minimum. If anything work related can be kept to weekdays, good. If not, make sure you take off a day in lieu when you can.

◆ Enjoy yourself!

Chapter Eight

Organising your man (without him realising it!)

RIGHT, LADIES, I'M GOING TO let you into a little secret: men think they are in control. Ha! Yes, I know it's ridiculous, but it's very important not to upset the apple cart by revealing the truth: that you are high empress of all things organisational (whether you want to be or not!). This chapter tells you how to handle this delicate situation.

Guy guidelines

If you're going to be a winning woman in the game of love, you need to set certain boundaries – and you need to train your man to obey them. This isn't as difficult as you might think, so be strong and consistent.

The most important rule

Don't let your man know that you are in charge. Yes, you have to take the reins if you want to get anything done – but he can't know it! You need to learn how to steer your man in the right direction without him realising it. In any situation, think of three options that you would be satisfied with, such as when choosing a takeaway on a Friday night. Think to yourself, 'I could handle pizza, a kebab or an Indian meal.' Then take these options to your guy – don't mention fish and chips, a Chinese or hamburger. Your man can choose from your pre-approved three and everyone's a winner: he thinks he's the king of Friday night, you're happy with the outcome. The 'Pick-three Programme' works with everything from holiday destinations to type of carpet – and normally promotes a very happy (balanced) relationship.

Choose your battles

You can't have everything your way (even if your man isn't aware you're winning on some things). Some things aren't worth the power struggle – they come with the man. Do organise him:

- To trim his nails and eyebrows (why should you be stuck with a hobbit?).

- To get his haircut regularly (see above).

- To make sure he treats you with the respect you deserve.

- To keep your relationship healthy.

- To help you manage your home and commitments.

Do not bother trying to organise:

- His 'weekends away with the boys'.

- His wallet.

- His computer desktop.

- His football fixture list.

- Putting the toilet seat down (it's not worth the effort – it won't happen).

Why do men feel the need to be chief organiser?

Women would like to be the most beautiful people in any given room; men would like to be the most powerful. With this power should come the ability to coerce people, rule situations and make decisions. Yes, to be the organised one. Men like to think (in their 18th-century heads) that women rely on them for guidance, strength and commonsense. Men want to be wanted, needed. In fact, they like to be seen as knights in shining armour. Why else do they fall at the feet of those clever women who have the little-girl-lost act down to a T?

Helping him to help himself

To find yourself suddenly partnered with the organisational equivalent of a loose-fitting kaftan (flimsy, transparent and out of date) can be frustrating for an efficient modern girl. Suddenly, you spend more time worrying about him than worrying about yourself. We sort his life out for him – basically, to make his life stress-free and more pleasant – and then, the insult of it all, we get criticised for nagging! Nagging! Do we want to spend our time repeatedly asking the same question? No, we'd rather be listening to Westlife in the bath, thank you very much, but they seem to need looking after. Grow up and organise yourselves, and the 'nagging' will stop, dear boys.

Mother syndrome

Some men like to be organised. They don't want the outside world to know it, of course, but inside your little twosome, they are quite happy for you to take over. It means less work for them, you see. Some women like this (to be organised, to feel needed, to stop her man ruining himself), but be careful not to turn into that thing no lover should turn into – duh duh duh, HIS MOTHER!

Ten signs you are overly organising/caring for him are:

1. Without thinking, you clear up after him in the bathroom – picking wet towels and dirty pants off the floor and putting them where they should be.

2. He asks you where his wallet is – and you know.

3. He asks you where his socks are – and you get up to find them for him.

4. He doesn't thank you any more for doing little things for him.

5. You remind him of his mother (and he tells you!).

6. You call or email his mother for him because he doesn't have the time.

7. You pretend to think it's cheeky or sweet when he's three hours' late home (he's drunk and the dinner is burnt), but a volcano of sadness is welling up inside you.

8. Even when you need attention, he expects you to give the cuddles/back tickles/advice.

9. You're paying a bill he's forgotten to sort out … again!

10. You feel like a bit of a mug – without the biological strings to help you get over it.

Say no to this, women of the world. Unless he wants to start paying you to be his personal assistant, housekeeper, psychologist and life coach, stop doing everything for him. He is not a child. And you will start to resent him eventually, which is the death knell to any healthy relationship.

NB Many men are expected to be highly bossy, scary and demanding at work, so when they get home they just want a quiet life and for someone else to make decisions for them. If you don't mind taking charge, brilliant! This can work. But set some ground rules: he cannot complain about your decisions, your choices or your way of doing things. And he must certainly never moan to his mates that you've chopped his balls off. He allowed you to!

How to make mutual decisions

Rather than spending time worrying, redoing plans or arguing, the key to organising your man is to get the options out there and make a decision that best suits both of you. Try the Pick-three Programme, or if it can't be as simply decided, take it in turns. Yes, that's right, decide together that if you're going to watch a Pink Floyd documentary one night, it's only fair he sits through a Kylie on tour DVD with you afterwards. And yes, that means without tutting, moaning or reading the paper noisily through it. All is fair in love and organisation. Get into the flow of taking it in turns and you might both actually start to enjoy each other's favourite things – and spend more quality time together.

THE PERFECT HOUSEWIFE

Sometimes, the woman should become chief organiser, social diarist, cleaning lady, laundrette and financial planner – if it has been agreed that she will be the one in that role. If her job is to stay at home and look after 'the family' then she will be expected to take on more of the above. Even so, she still deserves respect and thanks – and time off. If he becomes the househusband while you're the working girl, he will be expected to do more of the above. If, however, you are working the same hours under the same stress that he is, don't be a fool. Don't always be the one to unload the dishwasher. Set up a rota to share tasks.

Job seeker

If you want someone to organise you, date a man in one of the following professions – it comes naturally to them:

◆ The army, air force, or navy

◆ A celebrity publicist or manager

◆ A chef

◆ A personal trainer

◆ An accountant

Do not date:

◆ A philosopher

◆ An author (especially an unpublished one!)

◆ A 'pot-grower'

◆ A manager who has more than one personal assistant

◆ A celebrity – however Z list

ANDREA, 32

❝ My husband and I often complain that we both need a wife to organise our lives. We both have high-pressure jobs in the city with a long commute. This really eats into our time and means we rely on takeaways and cleaning ladies. We'd love to get home early and cook healthy meals for each other but it's just never going to happen – until one of us takes a step down the career ladder, anyway. So many modern couples must feel like this – the husband needs a wife, and the wife needs a wife! ❞

Organising his life

Taking on board all of the above rules on pushing him too hard, not pushing him enough and not becoming his mother, we're now going to go through the areas of his life where you can improve his day-to-day existence (and therefore your own).

Work

No one really knows what his or her partner is like at work. We may meet a few colleagues, get a tour of his office and attend the company dinner and dance once a year, but we don't know what he's like in meetings or what his boss really thinks of him.

When a woman becomes seriously interested in a man, she becomes invested in his future – it's natural. A biological thing kicks in where we weigh up how this man could provide for our (as yet) unborn children. So, suddenly, he's not just a boyfriend but also the man to put a roof over your head and food into your mouth – and his prospects at work become more attractive than a six-pack and looking good in a pair of jeans.

Without becoming a pushy girlfriend or wife, you can do little things to help your man organise his way to becoming a big boss:

◆ **Listen without prejudice.** Make a rule that you will spend the first hour of your time together – be it commuting home or when making dinner – to discuss any work worries. Listen, think and then offer unbiased, clear advice. Don't just throw up quick-fire solutions, but ask him questions so that he can explore what he really wants or needs. Make sure he does the same for you. It's amazing what you will learn from each other's situations – and how listening to someone from outside the office can give a fresh and interesting perspective. After you've had this hour, stop talking about work. Don't let it eat into your 'couple time'.

◆ **Offer 'beauty' advice.** Men aren't the best at general grooming. They may fiddle with the hair on their head for hours in the mirror (much to your chagrin!) but they don't pay such attention to the hair protruding from their ears, nostrils or collar. They can also go to work with shaving cuts, disgusting spots and dirty fingernails without a care in the world. No, no, no! – this trollism must end! Give them the facts in no uncertain terms: women find poor grooming vomit inducing, and it would not give your smart male boss a good impression of you either. If you live together, help his grooming along by keeping your bathroom shelves stocked with the essentials: tweezers, nail clippers, deodorant, ear cotton buds, spot cream, moisturiser, lip balm and shower gel. They'll soon take more pride in their appearance, which will give them a confidence boost in the workplace.

◆ **While we're on such shallow things as appearance,** help out your man by running his stuff to the dry cleaners when you take your own (and then organise him into returning the favour on alternate weeks), and if you can bear it, go shopping with him to make sure his shirt and tie combos are correct and flattering, and that his suit is a good fit. Too big and he'll look like a 1980s throwback; too small and he'll look like the office pervert. Remind him how important shoes are, too. My Great-great Aunt Joyce says you can judge a man by his shoes – and this can be the case in job interviews, too! Keep them neat and polished, and replace when you need to. Shoes should never be stacked, shiny or ridiculous.

◆ **Help him to organise a dinner party for his bosses.** If he thinks it would help, don't snarl and grumble at the idea of co-hosting an event. Showing he's an all-round good bloke and a capable host (with an amazing girlfriend) are all good things to highlight to your bosses and clients. You should concentrate on charming the wives and girl-friends of your guests.

◆ **When you're doing your own checklist** in the morning before you run out of the door, say it out loud to remind your beloved, too. Do I have any meetings I need to look extra smart for? Have I got a work do after work that I need to take casual gear for? Have I got my laptop? Do I need to get cash out?

◆ **Suggest that it would be fun** to embark on a course together – on a subject that could benefit you both, or give you an extra qualification. Think languages, com-puter skills or management/confidence boosters.

> **JOANNA, 33**
>
> ❝A friend and I discovered we shared the same problem with our husbands: they couldn't put their clothes in the dirty washing basket; they could only manage the floor next to the bed where they took them off. We joked that we should put the laundry basket on their side of the bed and maybe some clothes might accidentally fall into it. We tried it out and, low and behold, the majority of dirty clothes do now find their way into the basket.❞

Fitness

When you're planning a romantic weekend with your other half, working out probably doesn't come top of your list, but exercising produces endorphins and a natural high – and if they hit you both at the same time, kapow! You'll be running straight from the gym to your bedroom. You don't want a partner who is lazy, negative and out of shape, so organise him into getting fit with you.

Tell him the benefits a good workout will have on your sex life – that should get him going. Tell him exercise is a kind of foreplay and that you love to see his muscles flex and to watch him sweat. You don't have to stick to just the boring gym. Organise a romantic country walk, attend a dance class, and go skiing, skating or kayaking, play a game of tennis or go bowling with friends. Persuade him with five more top reasons:

1. You'll lose weight; his suit will fit him better.

2. You can have some quality time together that doesn't involve talking about your feelings.

3. Having someone by your side reduces the boredom factor of exercising.

4. Men like healthy competition – challenge him to beat a girl!

5. Promise him a massage if he strains a muscle!

Finances

Money, money, money … isn't so funny when you're dating a man with holes in his pockets and nothing in his bank account. I'm not suggesting you find yourself a Donald Trump, or indeed that you need a wealthy man to make you happy, but someone who has good sense when it comes to debt, loans and saving is a must. Otherwise, if you're an organised person like me, their lack of money sense will weigh heavily on your mind (and therefore, when you start trying to help them financially, your purse). Before it gets that bad, offer some non-threatening advice:

◆ Offer to sit down and go through his incomings and out-goings to see where savings can be made.

◆ Tell him if you've discovered a more efficient electricity supplier, cable-television service or credit card. Physically give him the leaflets so that he can't say he doesn't have the details.

◆ Go Dutch. Don't expect him to pay for everything then moan that he's in debt.

◆ Men have a tendency to file their bank statements in the bin. Buy him a (masculine) box to store all his financial documents in.

◆ If you live together, set up a joint bank account that you put equal amounts into each month. Spend a few hours when you first do this to organise direct debits – taking money automatically from both your accounts and paying off shared bills. Also, use this card for supermarket shopping and home improvements.

◆ Quietly question big spending. Does he really need a projector, skiing trip with the boys and a new car? Tease him. Say, 'You can have all that if you take me away to Bermuda for the weekend first', or, 'Well, if you're doing that, I'm buying that very expensive wedding dress I saw with my mother!' That'll make him think twice.

◆ If you trust him and you have the money, pay off a debt with ridiculous interest rates for him – and arrange a sensible payback time. But don't make a habit of it; just do it to get him out of a ridiculous over-paying situation. You are not his piggy bank.

◆ Lead by your example. Agree to pull your belts in together in January, for example. Cut out the late-night takeaways and boozing sessions. Stay in and cook, drink from your wine collection and head to the cinema rather than to expensive events.

◆ If he has an expensive and unhealthy habit – from smoking to pot-holing to smoking pot, encourage him to give up.

NB Don't emasculate your man! In his weird head when you talk about his bank balance, you could be talking about the size of his penis. Be kind, not too judgemental and understand things such as paying for MBAs, student loans or wayward sisters.

Family

You can't get too involved here. He and his family will have a wealth of issues and dramas that you couldn't and shouldn't get involved in. If he doesn't want to spend time with them, don't push it without knowing the details. If it's just general disorganisation that is stopping him from being a good son/ grandson/brother, though, you are more than welcome to step in once you get to know his family.

Without scaring him into thinking you're getting too close too quickly, get contact details for his family so that you can take over making arrangements. When his mother calls the house, don't avoid her call or cut the conversation short. Offer to have the family over, or ask when you'll next see her. Then put it in your partner's diary so that he can't complain he didn't know about your family plans.

It's not your responsibility to buy his family cards and gifts for Christmas and birthdays, but if you're feeling par- ticularly organised, when you're updating your diary, ask for his key family members' special days to add to yours – then email the week before to remind him to get off his arse and go shopping!

When it comes to getting him involved with your family, you really can't do much more than cross your fingers and hope they get on, or at least have an easy relationship where they don't mind spending a few hours together. Don't insist he spends every Saturday morning at your auntie's – pick the important things then emphasise how much you would like him there. Give him plenty of warning, remind him the day before and make the drive there and back as non- confrontational as possible – even if your mother was a bit annoying, don't take your stress out on him.

One of the biggest organisational dramas when it comes to families is the day you introduce your family to his. Now, you really should take charge of this: women are better at sensing where would be an appropriate location, what would be a good time and being sensitive to the situation. Wait until everyone involved feels ready. Don't insist on a big meeting on your three-month anniversary. The more natural the situation, the better.

When you get to know – and love – his family, don't insist you spend all your time with them if he doesn't want to. Alternatively, if you can't stand his family, try to keep a lid on it even if you think he'd agree with you. It is an undeniable truth that while you can slag off your own family, it's not acceptable for anyone else to!

If you can lightly sort him out on the family communication front, his family will bestow lots of praise on you – and the best way to do this is the simple things: reminding him to make phone calls, send cards and show up on time to family events. That's enough.

Retail therapy

If it can possibly be avoided, don't go shopping with men. Unless your fella has asked you to accompany him to offer fashion advice, which is quite sweet, leave this area well alone.

Clothes shopping

Some men make fabulous shopping companions but most don't. He knows how hideous high streets and shopping centres are on a Saturday – jam-packed with depressed women with muffin tops and credit-card problems! If you must go shopping together:

◆ Keep the trip short.

◆ Send him off on mini missions to keep him occupied.

◆ Warn him at the beginning that if you ask him if you look fat, the answer is no.

◆ Keep him on a leash. You don't want to waste time looking for him.

◆ Make use of him: let him park the car, carry your bags and bring you water.

Food shopping

It would be wonderful to send your man off to the supermarket, but as I know from experience, even when clutching a carefully written list, he'll come back with three bottles of fizzy pop, a bag of charcoal and a bumper pack of Monster munch. Useless!

If he insists, organise him by:

◆ Making it fun, set him challenges like on *Supermarket Sweep*.

◆ Keep him quiet by letting him put things in the trolley, but take the truly ridiculous things out when he's not looking.

◆ In fact, make sure you keep hold of the trolley/basket at all times.

◆ If he starts moaning, tell him to buy a newspaper and wait for you in the car – his groaning will slow you down.

◆ When you ask him to pick things up for you, check what he actually picks up. You would not believe the amount of well-meaning men who can't tell the difference between an aubergine and a courgette!

◆ If, after a visit, he agrees never to come with you again, milk the fact that he realises what a hassle it is. Make him do something around the house as payback for every time you have to head to the supermarket. When you're battling the crowded aisles, he can be doing the washing-up!

MEL, 36

❝ When Bill first moved in with me, we argued all the time over the washing-up, as we didn't have a dishwasher. I always ended up doing it and, unsurprisingly, it really annoyed me. During one argument, Bill said, "For God's sake, just buy a dishwasher and I'll pay for it." He then went away on business, so I bought a dishwasher and got a plumber round to install it. When he got home I handed him the bill. He was a bit surprised, but he paid it, and the arguments stopped. ❞

Romance and sex

Ah, good, now we're discussing something we can benefit from! The first way to organise your man is to get Valentine's Day (and other special occasions) sorted. Men can lack imagination, so send him subliminal messages: tell him you would love a Jo Malone surprise, tell him you've always wanted to eat at The Ivy, tell him you expect to be taken out on a certain night. And keep telling him! Leave info for future presents you'd like around the place (rip out pages from magazines or leave catalogues open at a certain page). Don't let him forget that he needs to romance you, and very soon being considerate will become second nature.

When he gets stressed at work, you will have to organise him into giving you time in the bedroom. Sex is the first thing that suffers when work pressures get too much. Keep the passion alive by looking after him, and gently bossing him around. Pull him into bed early before he falls asleep on the couch. Run him a hot bath and jump in with him. Set your alarm 30 minutes early so that he can't grumble that he'll be late when you try to get it on in the morning.

Men's magazines and 'lad's lit' are surprisingly good at educating men, who would happily resist the persistent requests from their better half for more romance and attention. Get him a subscription to *Men's Health* for Christmas – you'll soon notice him making more effort in the sack.

Boys aren't really up for subtle messages; if he needs to be more romantic, you're going to have to spell it out. If you want to have more sex, tell him loud and clear. If you need to organise a date night, do it. Be careful not to get in the way of footie practice or boys' night, and pick a date to put in the diary for together time every week. If he misses, he has to buy you a present and sort out an extra-special date within three days.

NB How can girls use the crying game to organise an improvement in their man? The key is not to turn on the waterworks too often. Men do respond to a woman's weeping and feel an urge to jump on their white stallion to rescue a woman in distress, but choose the right time and reason to pull out your best card. If you cry every time they come in late, you'll become 'the girlfriend who cried wolf' and your power will weaken. I've found it best to remember the smaller things and then collect them into one big weep – demanding improvements and changes or else. He'll be so keen to shut you up, he'll promise to get better – and so scared it will happen again, he probably will improve!

Are you fed up with organising?

I get this – I'm busy bossing people around and making decisions all week, and I want to spend the weekend being told what to do and not having to think too hard. I think this must explain my premature adoration for all-inclusive cruises and their planned itineraries. If you get tired of being the bossy mother to a teenage son, talk to him. Explain how you feel. He might think you're an organisational powerhouse who loves doing everything (yes, men do think this!). If you need more than words:

1. **Take a step back.** In which areas are you sorting him out without even realising it? Stop doing the small, unnoticeable stuff and he'll soon notice what you do and take it on board.

2. **Throw back the restaurant guide/phone/Yellow Pages** at him for once to plan your night.

3. **Chill out.** Neither of you make a decision! Take the day as it comes … if you can manage it.

4. **Don't keep the rota just for household chores.** Organise rotas for your whole life, from organising dinner dates with friends to choosing what you watch on the box.

5. **Dump him!** If it's getting to a stressful level, and you feel like a cross between Cinderella and one of her ugly sisters, this man is not for you – he's too lazy and immature. You deserve someone who can manage their own sock drawer … and who can be bothered to romance you properly.

When he turns Mr Organiser

Some women have the opposite problem from the above. As a couple settle into a unit and real personalities emerge (not the 'I'm perfect', honeymoon-stage personalities), some men can behave as if running their woman is like running a military operation. Yes, he can tell you to stop being late for dates and that you should manage to get yourself on time. Yes, he has every right to ask you to bring your own toiletries to leave at his flat because you are ruining all his razors when you stay over (it would be romantic if he bought you supplies, though, yeah?). And, he can even ask you not to chuck magazines and chocolate wrappers everywhere and to throw them in the bin instead.

A new relationship can be a good time to iron out your own foibles and flaws, and even more will be exposed when you move in together – you can look at this as another chance to straighten yourself up even more. So, if your man is trying to organise you for the greater good, well done him – he must like a challenge and a to-do list himself. What he can't do is try to change you or control you to the point that you become a mouse with a nervous issue.

◆ He can ask you to pick up your clothes off the floor; he can't pick out all your clothes for you.

◆ He can suggest you spend more time getting to know his friends; he can't suggest you get rid of yours.

◆ He can design the rota to make the household run smoother, but it must be fair and he can't scream or throw things if you forget a few things.

Be strong – recognise when you're being bullied and not being organised with the right intent.

Working together to organise a happy relationship.

Modern girls are natural plate spinners, and juggle a thousand things at once. Modern girls are also like girls throughout the ages: essentially nurturing, kind and peace-loving. Use your ability to plate-juggle with peace-loving motives at the root of it, and life should be good. Just make sure he is worth the effort before you invest your time, stress, money and heart. It's a too-often mentioned cry that one woman irons out the problems for another woman to come along later and benefit from! Repeat after me: 'I am not his mother, his slave, his personal assistant or his mug.'

Secrets of Success

◆ Be safe in the knowledge that most men secretly like to be bossed around. Think of all those stern secretary/nanny fantasies. Men even like the idea of being walked over by a woman in stilettos. Please, it's so obvious. If you can, be strict and sexy – that's the key.

◆ Organising him can seem like a challenge, but it will help you long term. For example, organise for him to take on the chores you hate, while taking on those things he doesn't like so much or do so well.

◆ If you're setting up a rota, put it on the fridge door – he can't say he hasn't seen it there.

◆ Make life as easy for him as you can when you first move in together: set up a filing system, empty boxes clearly labelled for him to put important things into, and set rules at the beginning.

◆ Make it clear from the start that you do not spend your time keeping a beady eye on his belongings. As fascinating as his wallet is, no, you haven't seen it. Cut out this insane questioning by putting a dump box near the front door that everything can go into.

◆ Don't patronise or do silly voices – that won't help you to get what you want.

◆ Rely on his sense of competition. Set him deadlines to do things by, or pitch him against you: if you can do this by Sunday, I'll do this.

◆ When he does toe the line and improve, reward him – with anything from sex to a roast dinner. Don't criticise how he's done it, just be grateful that he has. If you tell him off about how he's washed the dishes, he'll think, 'Why did I bother?'

◆ Organise time together. It's a common misconception that if you live together, you see each other all the time, so what's the point? Sorry, boys, no! Time spent tired in front of the box or cleaning the downstairs cupboard is not quality time. Organise date nights.

◆ All girls become naggers eventually, but do try to catch yourself. It's not an attractive trait. If he dares to call you a nag, reply, 'If you did what I asked the first, second or third time, you wouldn't have turned me into this!' Put it back on him!

◆ Analyse his relationship with his mother – you'll learn a lot about his opinions of women (what they should and shouldn't do, what they're in charge of, and so on) from observing her with him, or even talking about his childhood.

◆ Men are like sponges – they do take in routines, ideas and rules. If he's worth the effort, put it in. Even the laziest couch cuddler can become efficient and useful with the guidance of a good woman!

Chapter Nine

Planning the perfect party

B EING A SOCIAL BUTTERFLY sometimes requires you bringing the socialising home, and playing hostess with the mostest to your nearest and dearest. But even if it's just a simple supper party for a few close friends, it can be difficult to coordinate and make sure that everyone has a fun time. So this next chapter should help.

That's entertainment

Before you plan an event – of any size – that you will be hosting, consider the following:

◆ Do you have enough money to do the event properly? There's no point scrimping over the details if you're strapped for cash. It's better that you save up and do the event when you're financially more secure. And these things – even a dinner for four – are pricey.

◆ Do you have the time to set aside to plan a party? It's not a case of buying a few crates of beer and inviting people over on the night. No, no, no, you'll need to thoroughly clean every area where guests will go, and do a proper shop – it's not just booze and food, it's cleaning products, napkins, lemons and limes, and so on.

◆ Is it a good time of year to do it? If you're relying on outdoor space, you need to wait until summer (or take a chance with muddy carpets and steamed-up, damp guests). If you want everyone important to attend, choose a dull month; that is, not around Christmas or Valentine's Day weekend.

◆ Has it been agreed with your partner or flatmates? Always check that it's fine with the person you share space with. They may have other plans or not fancy a lot of drunken dancers making out in their bedroom.

◆ Why are you having the party? If it's because you think it will be fun, or it's a celebration or an exciting surprise for someone, go for it. If you're doing it to try to get your claws into a man you hope will attend, or to show off your new pad, things could backfire. Make sure you're having it for the right reason.

ROSEMARY, 45

❝ Some years ago an elderly aunt was coming up for her 80th birthday, so the family decided to give her a surprise party, at which she announced "But I'm not 80! I'm 79!" Both her sister and her daughter told her she'd got it wrong and ignored her protest. It was only six years later when she passed away that her daughter checked her birth certificate and realised she was right and we were wrong. Anyway, I think she enjoyed her premature party! ❞

Essential entertaining

Sometimes we can get lost in a whirl of tiny details when we're planning to have people over. We think too much about the fact that the front path needs re-paving, or that our bathroom has seen better days. But the truth is, rather than these small things, the emphasis should be on this: the guests. When planning a do of any size or level of importance, focus on:

◆ The food

◆ The drink

◆ The music

◆ The decorations, if needed

◆ The games and entertainment, if needed

You don't need people to come away from your event thinking, 'Wow, what a spectacular bathroom', although it would be lovely if they did! No, you want them to come away saying, 'Bloody hell, that was fun. I love that girl! I love her parties!'

TEN TIPS FOR BEING SOCIABLE ... WHEN YOU DON'T WANT TO BE!

You might not have organised for guests to come over, but suddenly there are some unwanted friends or family members at your door and you have to become very accommodating. Here are the basics:

1. Make your uninvited guests feel welcome by taking their coats, umbrellas and boots (if wearing them) as soon as they walk in.

2. Offer a drink to them within the first 15 minutes.

3. If it really is a bad time and you're busy or going somewhere, tell them from the start. That way, it won't look like an excuse. If you haven't got a concrete appointment but haven't got a few hours to waste socialising, be straight up: say you've had a busy week and you've got to do the laundry, but get your calendar out to set up a future planned date.

4. If smoker guests are fidgeting, offer an ashtray, or if yours is a non-smoking house, show them out to a patio and offer up a chair or an umbrella to make it a bit more comfortable.

5. Don't get so disorganised that your house is run to ruin. Make sure you never run out of toilet paper, soap, clean towels or clean mugs and glasses.

6. Don't put the television on and stare at it zombified with guests present. Set your video to catch any programme you want to watch, unless it's something you think they'll like, too.

7. Try to maintain some state of personal decency between 11.00 a.m. and 9.00 p.m. Outside those hours (and rainy Sundays), pyjamas are acceptable, or even a dirty old tracksuit and greasy hair. But when guests could knock – or even the neighbours – try not to be naked, dirty or smelly.

8. This is hard to do when you're really busy, but a few groceries can stop you stressing if someone suddenly appears at your front door. Milk in the fridge is a must, with tea and coffee in the cupboard, of course. A bottle of wine is a great plus, too. If you can resist bingeing during moments alone, biscuits and nuts are fab to have stored as well.

9. If you have sudden overnight guests, tell them to make themselves at home (that is, get themselves water, take showers) and always keep spare clean sheets and towels so that you don't have a sudden laundry panic.

10. Thank them for visiting. Even if it was a shock and a bit of a hassle, don't let them feel it!

What kind of party are you having?

No two parties are made the same. The time of year, reason for celebrating and number of guests all change the event dramatically.

Dinner parties

They take a tremendous amount of, er, cooking – unless you hire in caterers (which isn't as expensive as you'd think) or get it all frozen and prepared from Marks & Spencer (delicious and easy, and also not as expensive as you'd think). Guests will love that you are 'cooking' and hosting a delightful meal – it makes them feel exclusive and special, and these meals allow for good conversation and really getting to know people.

On the day, check that napkins and cutlery are clean, plus the house and your quick I'm-the-cook outfit. Draw up a seating plan, if you think it's best. Think about candles and/or flowers for table decorations, and perhaps invest in some fun board games for afterwards.

NB Aim to enjoy your own bashes – your enthusiasm and enjoyment will shine through, reflect on the event and inspire your guests to feel the same. Don't take on such a major task that by the time the day arrives you are fraught with stress, exhausted from sleepless nights, and looking like a drug-addled bag lady twice your age from worry! Enjoy yourself.

Cocktail parties

These can be pricey, as you will normally invite about 50 people if at your home, or 100 if you've hired somewhere. Everyone needs to be fed and watered. The most important rule to set here is the time: don't make it an all-nighter, as it will break the bank. Make it a firm 7.00–9.00 p.m. If people want to carry on drinking after that, it's at their own expense. Send out invites and ask to be informed of plus ones, and keep the music interesting, brave and upbeat.

ANDREA, 32

❛ I just love parties – I love everything about them, going to them, organising them for work and having my own at home. Two years ago when my husband and I moved into our new home we thought: how shall we budget? And, what's more important, a new kitchen, or converting the cellar into a permanent nightclub, complete with bar, dance floor and karaoke machine? You can guess which won. And it's great 'cause we never worry about our house being trashed, as we can access the cellar from a side path in the garden. It's the talk of our town! ❜

Special parties

Be it a birthday party, or a wedding, a divorce or a christening party, make it stand out. People are invited to so many parties these days, it has to be a good one to get them off their sofas. Be original. Pick themes and have fun with the decor. Hire in entertainers (singers, dancers, acrobats, celebrity look-alikes, artists, and so on). At midnight, serve bacon butties and cups of tea to keep the party going ... and make sure that all guests leave with a goody bag or at least a slice of cake (it will take them back to their childhood, which is always a good thing).

PREPARE FOR THE UNEXPECTED

Even if you and your guests are having a wonderful time, things can go wrong: I've had friends locked in the bathroom for hours, different friends spray-painting the same bathroom with vomit and a friend getting their arm stuck in the letterbox while performing a magic trick (the fire brigade were called and no long-term damage done). Have on hand in case of emergencies:

- Basic medical kit

- Hangover cures and headache tablets for the morning after

- An assortment of cleaning products

- A clean spare room and towels in case someone needs to stay over

- Numbers for local taxi firms and details of last trains

Party planner extraordinaire

Organisational skills are a social butterfly's must-have! When you start to sort out your event you need to think ahead and do the following:

1. **Set the date asap.** If you're choosing a Saturday night, this is especially important. Give guests warning. If it's a huge event like a wedding, or a party abroad, I even suggest sending 'save the date' cards before the invites themselves. These cards also build buzz, mystery and excitement. Whatever you do, though, don't invite people just a few days before an event – they will feel like last-minute add-ons or replacements.

2. **Keep a guest list.** Make a note of everyone you've invited, plus their plus ones, and so on, and update the master list when acceptances, refusals and requests for extra invites come in. That way you'll know roughly how many people to cater for (keep in mind that there are always no-shows on the night).

3. **Plan food and drink.** How many people are coming, how many canapés do you need per person (I recommend ten each) and how many cocktails will they consume each (I recommend four)? Account for different tastes and needs; for example, do a few vegetarian options – and remember to buy soft drinks, juices and water. Also, think about those finishing touches such as lemons and limes, ice and herbs – plus chocolates and nibbles in dishes scattered around the place.

4. **Do a party plan.** Map out your area and decide where the makeshift bar will be, where you'll set out the food (near the kitchen) and where you'll erect the poles for exotic dancing. This will help you decide where to put extra chairs and/or if you need to move furniture out to clear more space. Don't have everything in one spot – spread the food, drink and dancing out to keep people circulating and mingling.

5. **Party-proof your home** (if having the event there). Remove all personal, embarrassing and valuable objects from conspicuous places. Hide dangerous things away from drunken hands. Don't worry too much about going on a cleaning frenzy before the party – people won't notice dusty corners – as you'll need to do a proper clean-up the day after (bathrooms are the only exception, they need to be spotless for guests). Provide napkins and coasters where food and drink are served, and set up a storage centre near the front door for coats and shoes.

6. **Set yourself a party diary.** It will be impossible to do everything on the day of the event (remember you need to leave time to turn yourself into a dazzling doyenne too!), so you'll need to timetable the preparation time over the course of a few days. Think through everything you'll need to do (clean, shop, blow up balloons, and so on) and how long, realistically, it will take. Then double the time to allow for mishaps.

7. **Make an effort.** Go that extra step further. It's easy to offer a few drinks and nibbles, but if you organise your time properly – and allow yourself enough time to do research – you can make your party an original, something to set the standard. Hit the Internet for great ideas for themes and decorations, and ask friends what their best nights out have been, and what they included.

8. **Plan your budget.** Decide where you want your cash to go. If you want to hire a cool DJ that will cost a fortune, think about asking people to bring a bottle to save on drinks costs. Investigate cheap ideas that have instant impact, such as fairy lights, metallic confetti sprinkled on surfaces, using mirrors as drinks trays, serving childhood favourite food that's easy and reasonable to serve, such as penny sweets, jam sandwiches, cheese and pineapple sticks and pickled-onion Monster Munch!

9. **Let go, party hard.** Spend the hour before the party getting ready – as the hostess you should look gorgeous, so make the effort. Then 15 minutes before kick-off, open a bottle of champers or shake yourself a mai tai to sip while doing a final look-round. Ask a few of your best friends to arrive on time so that you can get going without worrying if anyone is going to show up … and then stop fussing, let your hair down and enjoy it! Entertaining friends and family is one of life's greatest pleasures – and treasures!

10. **If something does go wrong** (such as bad weather halving your guest list or the caterer not showing up), don't beat yourself up. If a guest behaves naughtily or clumsily, don't make them feel embarrassed or stupid – the sign of a great hostess is how she responds to these social dramas. Think on your feet (so don't get too drunk until halfway through an event), smile, laugh and think what great party stories you'll have to tell in the office on Monday.

JANE, 39

❝Last year I had to organise an office party. Apart from nearly having a nervous breakdown, I enjoyed it. I had a folder and a long list to keep track of everything: venue, DJ, gifts, food, photographer, drinks, raffle prizes and table decorations. Once the venue was sorted, I booked everything, ticking off my list as I went. My only mistake was deciding – in my infinite wisdom – to make the ladies' gifts myself: to hand paint champagne flutes. The 200 painted glasses went down very well and the evening was a great success – but never again!❞

The well-planned guest list

A party is often a great success because of the mix of people present, so it's important to think carefully about who to include and how many.

◆ If you want a low-key, chilled-out do, only invite good friends and sociable easy-going newcomers. This will take the pressure off you.

◆ If you're planning a dinner party, don't invite three couples who know each other well plus one new, out-of-the-loop couple. They will feel excluded by in-jokes and unknown names, and this could become dull very quickly. Do an all-old-friends' dinner party, or mix it up a bit.

◆ Don't panic too much about seating plans – I presume you don't know any truly hideous freaks that need to be kept away from people over an exquisite meal, do you?

◆ Warn other guests if you have invited someone who has a sore spot or tough topic that's better not referred to; for example, a recent divorce or death in the family.

Being the best

It's not just about having a bottle of champagne in one hand, and a tray of delicious canapés in the other, being a top hostess is also about avoiding these faux pas:

◆ Not introducing guests to one another. Assume everyone needs a name reminder.

◆ Letting guests have an empty glass for too long.

◆ Accepting offers of help in the kitchen, and then treating your good guest like a galley slave while you bugger off to where the action is.

◆ Hiding the good wine and chocolate that guests have brought and serving some luke-warm bile you got at cut price.

◆ Making a drama out of clearing up. Leave it until morning. You don't want your guests to feel they need to stop gossiping or dancing and grab a tea towel.

Wake me up before you go-go

Revive flagging guests by spicing things up a bit. No one wants a bash to finish before midnight, but if it looks like yours is going that way, drastic measures are needed. Keep the booze coming and start experimenting with crazy cocktails; pump up the stereo with some 1980s classics or handbag house music; get your camera or video out – people will be flattered and want to look their best and most exciting; pay people compliments and open some windows; serve some delicious snacks and grab people up to dance!

Being a firm mistress to naughty, naughty guests

Not all guests are created equally. Some are perfect, bringing an abundance of joy, laughter and alcohol into your home, whereas others bring their problems and sod all. Don't be dismayed; here's how to handle them:

◆ Send the drunk and disorderly to bed, and the put the raucous in a taxi cab (you'll have to order it, they won't want to leave!).

◆ Defuse an argument between guests by dragging them apart subtly ('You must come and see a new dress I've just bought, it's upstairs!') or sending a friend round with some nibbles to interrupt them.

◆ If guests are late, and food is burning and stomachs are rumbling, get on with your event as if they don't exist. Put the needs and wants of the ones polite enough to show up on time first. If they ring ahead and explain, save them a plate and a party bag. If they don't, offer their portion round as seconds! And if they show up, give them what's left and a drink ... but don't let it ruin your evening.

◆ If guests arrive too early (you're in you knickers and bra and defrosting the garlic bread) shove them in a room and forget about them (just leave them with a drink and the remote control) or don't feel bad organising them into helping out with last-minute chores – it's their fault they've shown up before they're welcome!

◆ If guests show up empty-handed, drink you dry, and then leave without saying thanks, there's only one thing to do: cross them off your party invite list forever. Their loss.

Secrets of Success

◆ Make a list of people who you want to introduce to each other, or who you think would get on. Work out chances for them to meet through you.

◆ If you're throwing a drinks party, remember to eat something beforehand or all your organisational skills will go out of the window.

◆ Don't be a tight arse – if you want to entertain, you gotta spend.

◆ The white-wine-on-red-wine rule (for accidents with red wine on the carpet) does have some basis in truth, but you'll need lots of salt and a carpet cleaner to get rid of the stain completely.

◆ If someone has invited you to lots of things, repay the compliment. Three dinners maximum, then you need to start cookin' and hostin', girl!

◆ Do make the effort to look good. Get your hair done the day before if you're worried about time. And wear jewels and glitter – hey, you're the hostess with the mostest ... you can do whatever you like!

Chapter Ten

Preparing for high days and holidays

CONSIDERING TIME OFF FROM work is supposed to be fabulous and relaxing, we sure as hell get a bit stressed when the time arrives. Planning Christmas sends us straight into the January blues, and going on a trip to the sun can bring us out in packing-anxiety hives. Here's how to make the most of the best times in life.

How to have a successful festive season

Christmas is, of course, associated with stables, donkeys and the little baby Jesus, but it's also a universal time for spending time with loved ones, having a few days out of the office and a few days off your healthy-eating plan! Let's face it, there's nothing too pious about getting tipsy on sherry and burying yourself in a tin of chocolates. So enjoy this season – whatever your religion – and make the most of the giving and receiving of gifts!

The first rule is to remember what this time of year is all about: to have fun, enjoy being with your family and friends, relish the opportunity to eat too much and, whatever your outlook on religion and the thereafter, to think about how lucky you are and to make the most of life. Right, that's the moral, life-affirming bit out of the way – let's get practical. The same rules apply for the serious planning of any big event.

Start planning in July

Why not begin thinking about your perfect yuletide early on in the year. Leave it until 21 December and you'll be too harassed and knackered to care too much about the finer details that can make Christmas so much fun. Let's face it, if you're rushing around the shops pushing senior citizens and children into fir trees, you're not in the right frame of mind to pay attention to table decorations and the hand-stitched stockings.

◆ So, as soon as you like, start cutting out pictures or tips that you spot in books and magazines. Even ideas for other festivals, or general home decor tips, can offer inspiration. Start a Christmas folder and put all your cuttings and ideas in there.

◆ Lots of people buy the basics straight after Christmas, when the prices dramatically tumble immediately after Boxing Day. I used to think this was silly, storing up bits and pieces for a whole 12 months. Last year I tested this theory: I bought a cupboard full of cards, wrapping paper, crackers and other little trinkets such as decorations and candles. Yes, it took up a bit of room, but I stored them neatly, and you know what? It's sad, but when you get older 12 months fly by and, before I knew it, I was getting the box out and was so happy with my purchases and the money I'd saved! I had truly luxurious, decadent items but at a fraction of the price the same things were in the shops for in November! Hoorah – good planning!

◆ With all the socialising, food, drinks, presents (and new outfits), this is always an expensive time of year. So that it doesn't hit you and your bank manager too hard, open a separate bank account just for high days and holidays, and direct debit a certain amount into the account every month. Treat it as dead money until you need to play Mrs Claus!

◆ If you see the perfect gift, don't waste time, don't procrastinate – buy it immediately, otherwise you will forget. I saw a great gift for my friend Billy a few months ago. I couldn't be bothered to queue so told myself, 'I'll be back', and left the shop. Guess what? I haven't been back, I haven't got him a gift, and now I'm panicking!

◆ Make a list of what you've bought and what you can use again when you're packing away your Christmas things, so that you can be organised without needing to unpack everything when you start the next year – and so you don't overbuy or double up on anything.

◆ Buy gifts when you're on your travels somewhere on holiday. The treasures you find will be unique, personal and, with luck, no one else will have bought the same thing. And don't worry if you don't have a particular friend in mind. If something is beautiful and useful, everyone will want it.

◆ Remember: colds and flu can take out the healthiest person in the winter, so it's good to plan. That way, you can wallow in self-pity under a duvet without panicking that you have too much to do! If you're lucky enough to live in the southern hemisphere, watch out for heatstroke as well as a burnt turkey!

KATIE, 27

❝ I have a running list of people in my head that I have to buy presents for. As soon as I see something they'll like, I buy it – even if it's in the summer! If your friend mentions that she wants to learn to paint, buy her a canvas and easel that day. She'll be so impressed you remembered when she opens the gift in December. Also when Christmas rolls around, most of your shopping will be done and you can relax and enjoy what the holiday is really about – eating and drinking! ❞

Shopping with minimum hassle

Undoubtedly the biggest pain in the ass during the festive season is shopping. Battling to find a space in a car park, fighting through the crowds with tons of bags, bitching your way to the last pair of slippers in a packed-out shop – yuk! But you can make life easier for yourself.

As well as planning early, as we've discussed, plan good! Make a list of everyone you need to buy for – and don't forget birthdays that fall around the festive season, too. When you're buying those presents, buy birthday cards and paper as well. Don't just wish them happy birthday in their Christmas card, and wrap their gifts in red and green. That's thoughtless!

CATHERINE, 33

❝ Be strict with yourself and write at least three shopping days into your diary now! And don't cancel those dates. Plan these days for October or November, then pencil in another day for wrapping the gifts, and another day for writing Christmas cards. Make it more fun by indulging in your favourite Christmas drink while you're doing the chores (Bailey's all the way!) and play Christmas carols or watch *A Wonderful Life* to remind you why you're going through all this hassle! ❞

When you're deciding what to buy for people, be realistic. If you're skint, don't overspend. No one wants you to get into debt so that they have something under the tree.

Also, it sounds mean but remember what people bought you last year. There's no point in embarrassing them and crippling yourself with your generosity. This also works vice versa – if a friend is particularly generous and thoughtful, pay her gift extra attention. It will save your cringes at exchanging point!

On the day of a big shop, dress for comfort. Wear comfortable shoes and layers – easy to take off as you rush from the outdoors into the stores. Glamour is not an option. I shop in tracksuits and trainers. I'd even go so far as to wear a rucksack. Hey, you need to keep your hands free!

Shop with a friend; it will help with choosing things, especially if she has good taste, and you can keep yourself motivated by having a fancy lunch together halfway through your list. But make sure she doesn't just drag you where she needs to go. If you have to split up and meet for coffee after a few hours of solo shopping, do that.

Saturday shopping is totally time-consuming and depressing. The world and his mother will be queuing up to pay for gifts with you. If you have an extra day's holiday to take before the end of year, use it to go shopping and make an event of it. Head out to a large out-of-town shopping centre, or into the glamorous heart of a big city. During the week, shopping is much calmer and quieter, so you can get your stuff done in half the time.

Don't make yourself ill. Carry water to stay hydrated and remember to eat. Stop every few hours to chill out and check your list. Reward yourself with a hot foot soak and a takeaway when every last perky person is ticked off your list.

TOP TEN EXCELLENT (AND EASY) PRESENT IDEAS

1. If you've read a fabulous book this year, buy it for all your friends and write a special message to each one inside it – leading them to a particularly poignant moment that they would relate to. Wrap it in brown paper and string, like an old-fashioned bookshop would!

2. For a very special lady, organise a year's worth of flowers to be delivered over the next 12 months. A bouquet per month is affordable and it's a gift that keeps on giving. What woman doesn't adore flowers?

3. Christmas stockings aren't just for kids. Buy jaunty, knitted ones for every member of your family then head to a large chemist to fill them up with mini bottles of beauty products, lip balms, hair bands, make-up, shower gels and chocolates!

4. Save time – and provide fun – by buying a family group a selection of board games to share.

5. Everyone loves a cup of coffee in the morning. Put coffee-shop vouchers in your Christmas cards for a caffeine surprise!

6. If the true gift of Christmas is giving, make a one-off charitable donation on behalf of all your friends and family – and write the details of this, and where to go to help more, inside a card.

7. Book a group manicure at your favourite salon for the girls, and get tickets to a football or rugby match for the boys. That way, they get the fun of opening it – and the fun of actually doing it, too. And don't forget to book yourself a manicure along with the others!

8. Cashmere is a true luxury and always wanted. Buy close friends cashmere covers for hot water bottles, buy colleagues cashmere socks, and your granny a cashmere jumper.

9. Let someone else do the work for you. Head to a perfumery, pick your favourite scents and let the trained staff there choose an alluring selection of matching products and wrap them in their impressive-looking boxes with ribbons. They'll look fabulous under the tree – especially if you get your whole family things from the same shop.

10. Get fine wines and cheeses delivered in a hamper. Find local or organic businesses on the web and get the hampers sent to your loved ones' homes the week before Christmas. Everyone wants to go gourmet during the festive period.

NB DIY presents seem like a good idea, but be careful! Follow instructions, make sure you have all the right equipment and materials, and have a dry run. Don't start making cups and saucers in your local pottery studio on Christmas Eve, if you want your dad to be happy! Going homemade can also cost more and take more time than you'd think – if your plan backfires you'll end up having to go out and buy gifts as well. That's a waste of time and money. Homemade gifts with a chance of succeeding include hand-painted vases and candlesticks, cookies and brownies with special personal messages written in icing, and favourite photos put onto mugs or mouse mats.

Wrap stars

Don't under-buy! When you first head out to do your shopping, buy more paper than you think you need and buy it all in the same two colours so that you can mix and match, and a theme will build. At this point, buy a decent pair of scissors (the wrong kind will really slow you down), matching ribbons and name tags and lots of Sellotape – the stuff where the end is easy to find. If you can get your partner to help, that's a good thing, too – probably half the stuff you're wrapping is for his side of the family anyway, huh!

Once you've wrapped, get the gifts into the hands of the right people as soon as possible. If you're spending Christmas with your family, take the presents round to place under their tree at the beginning of December, if they live nearby. It'll look lovely – and exciting as you see the gifts build up!

Save on postage (which can cost more than the actual presents!) and last-minute mad driving dashes, by being organised enough to hand out gifts to friends from November onwards.

KATHERINE, 26

❝If you're planning a Christmas party but don't want to stress out about decorating and looking festive enough, hold a "naked tree" party. All your friends bring hand-made decorations. This will save you time and give you a memorable tree. Set out equipment and materials and get friends to make mini fairy versions of themselves. When people get tipsy, the decorations get hilarious. This can also be done at Easter – throw a "paint an egg" brunch!❞

Delightful decor

Decorating your home for the yuletide lifts the spirits and warms the heart – it doesn't have to raise the panic levels.

◆ **Store things properly.** On the twelfth day of Christmas wrap delicate baubles in tissue paper or individual plastic bags and place carefully in a box. Pack it full and tape it shut so that nothing can move. Write what you've placed in each box on the side so that you won't forget what's in what when it's time to get festive again.

◆ **Colour-code your decorations** and store them separately so that it's easy to fulfil your theme dreams without hours of searching for the right things.

◆ **Don't get into a tangle** – wrap beads and tinsel around used wrapping-paper rolls to store them neatly.

◆ **You don't need to leave it until the last minute to decorate.** If you've got a lot on as the big day gets nearer, deck the halls on 1 December – who cares what the neighbours say!

◆ **If you haven't got lots of time,** keep it minimal and drape fairy lights on mantelpieces and banisters for instant twinkle.

◆ **Fake it, baby!** Real trees are difficult to buy, transport and keep off the carpet, so don't be forced by snobs into abandoning your trusty plastic one.

◆ **For classy, simple and cheap decorations,** sprinkle glitter and metallic confetti on surfaces and add some tea lights.

◆ **Use holly and mistletoe** for a country festive feel.

> **NB Are making your own decorations** a good idea or a waste of time and money? Well, if you've really got a doable concept, as well as the time to make them look lovely, that's fabulous. If they haven't turned out too well, however, pretend you got your friends' kids to make them. It may pay to keep it simple: glitter-spray pine cones; bake and glaze iced cookies; wrap tiny boxes and tie them with ribbon to the tree branches.

New Year's resolutions

One of the biggest pushes to organise yourself occurs in the minutes running up to a new year – where the future seems to hold extra motivation and promise.

I'm guilty of setting myself outlandish resolutions, breaking them on the sixth day and then feeling guilty to the point I overindulge in the bad things I was trying to stop! Set sensible resolutions – don't promise to give up all the things you love in one go. And if you are being good, allow yourself naughty tokens in case you mess up. Or even allow yourself the weekend off from your new year's regime of sanctimonious withdrawals.

If you do muck up, don't let it eat you up (as it has me too often) – start again. Start your resolutions over on 1 February. Alternatively, introduce cutbacks rather than total abstinence as your resolution on drinking, smoking, partying or indulging in chocolate.

Resolutions are great ways of getting your priorities straight, though. Stop and think what you really want to change. Take time (when sober) to plan how your life could be better. And remember: resolutions don't have to be about stopping the bad things – they can be about starting things, too. This year, mine were positive, 'soul food' resolutions: to be a better friend, to read more books and to dance on my own in the lounge whenever the mood takes me. And I've kept to all three of them!

Egg-static Easters!

Easter isn't just an important time of year in the Christian calendar but it also symbolises fresh starts and summer being only around the corner. Celebrate Easter weekend by:

◆ Making your own chocolate treats using moulds found in all good cook shops.

◆ Giving pots of Easter flowers to your nearest and dearest, and planting festive flowers in pots outside your front door.

◆ Hand-painting hard-boiled eggs, to use as decoration for a dinner party or to hide around the house and garden if you have kids who'd enjoy an egg hunt.

◆ Inviting friends over for a fondue night – complete with marshmallows and fresh fruit.

◆ Bake bunny- and chick-shaped cookies, and ice them in pastel colours to give to colleagues and friends.

How to enjoy your holiday

Sun, sea, sangria and possibly (safe) sex – what's not to like? Well, it's amazing the amount of people who get ill on holiday, as their body releases the pent-up emotions and stresses from months in the office. And of course, lots of people fight with their nearest and dearest, purely because they're not used to spending so much time with each other and the pressure is on to have constant fun!

Planning your trip

Here's how to sort the perfect holiday in ten easy steps:

1. First things first, can you get the time off work? There's no point dreaming if your boss is away and you need to hold the fort. Get dates cleared asap.

2. Don't get overexcited and over-invite. If this is supposed to be a romantic trip, don't drunkenly invite your best friend and her lout of a boyfriend.

3. Check a world weather map. You may have always wanted to go to Cuba, but if it's the stormy season, no amount of mojitos is going to make your holiday a salsa-swinging success.

4. Assess different types of accommodation. Is it worth spending the extra now to go all-inclusive? How much do you eat? Do you like to experiment with new cuisines? Are there local restaurants near the hotel? How expensive are restaurants in the town you're visiting? Would a villa suit your needs more, or do you want to be more looked after?

5. Buy a travel guide to get a better sense of the country, and send out an all-friends email asking for advice from people you know who have been there. Some of it may be a bit, 'Well, I've done India, and you must go to this tiny shack, blah, blah ...' but bear with it – there could be a gem in there!

6. Come up with a loose itinerary before you jet off. Include all the things you must do or you'll regret it forever after, as well as a few things to fill in a rainy day or an energetic night.

7. Double-check visa requirements – and what you are allowed to take in and bring out of the country. A week in the cells is not what you're after.

8. Make sure someone is around to keep an eye on your house/plants/pets/boyfriend while you're away, and leave clear notes to your colleagues outlining ongoing work projects. This will allow your mind to escape home totally and relax.

9. Enter the perfect packing zone a week before you travel. Decide what suitcase or bag you are taking and start filling it with essentials as you remember. Start your laundry now, too, so that it's all ready to go. Keep passports and tickets, plus other essentials (such as plug adaptors and insect repellent) somewhere safe and sound. And remember: less is more – you don't need a thousand jumpers if you're heading to a sunny clime. Be sensible, and take only your favourite things and the necessities. Think about taking half-empty bottles of shampoo, and so on – they can be tossed at the end of the trip to make way for bottles of local spirits and stuffed donkeys!

10. Finally, always take a camera – keep it on your person at all times when travelling, as you never know what you'll see. Remember to take batteries and film, and then develop or upload your images as soon as you get back, or you could lose them. And then what will you bore your friends with over dinner?

MELISSA, 26

❝ When I'm on vacation, I dress in just one or two colours. If I bring all black and white clothing, I can create more outfits out of fewer items and save space in my bag. You can also save space by rolling up small T-shirts, socks, undies and bras and stuffing them into shoes and nooks and crannies in your case. Oh, and when you've got to your destination – unpack asap and hang up creased items in the shower room. The steam trick is a good one! ❞

Things to avoid on holiday

There's nothing worse than being ill or confused in a foreign place. Limit sickly damage by packing a mini medicine kit, which includes painkillers, cough and cold remedies, indigestion/constipation/diarrhoea medicines, plasters and bandages. Read up on issues before you travel somewhere, and follow advice. If you're not supposed to eat the salads or drink the water, don't. If you have a sensitive stomach, bring some comfort food and drinks with you – be it tea bags from home or your favourite spread to have on dry toast.

If you do become sick, tell the hotel or travel representative asap. Whatever you do, don't wait for your situation to worsen. And, although it is a chore, sort out holiday insurance before you go. It will give you the confidence to skydive and scuba!

Another holiday nasty is getting into any kind of trouble: with the police, with other holidaymakers, with the locals. We'll assume you've done nothing wrong (seeing as you're a lovely modern girl), but if problems arise, don't take the law into your own hands. Ask your rep for help, or even the foreign embassy if you feel it's that serious. Remember to take necessary contact details with you on your travels.

Things to do to make your holiday even better

Organise yourself: read relevant books to get educated, watch relevant television shows to get excited and learn a few useful phrases and greetings to get you understood. When you arrive at your destination, make friends, by all means, but don't commit to spending every minute with them. And don't give them your home address and phone number, an email is sufficient. Holiday friends can soon lose their sparkle and you'll feel like you're being stalked if they call you at home suggesting weekends away together.

Save up before your holiday to have enough money to do everything you want to do. Sign up for every frequent-flier scheme and offer going. Those points do suddenly add up to an upgrade – and that is the best way to start a holiday.

Try to turn off from home as much as possible: tell your family you won't be checking in (just leave the resort's number in case of emergencies) and turn off your phone so that the office can't bother you. And remember: hangovers in the heat are hell – and a waste of valuable time. Indulge, but with care, because local spirits can really knock you for six.

Secrets of Success

◆ Buy personal knick-knacks whenever you see them. If you see cute napkins or key rings with initials, names or relevant places on them, stock up!

◆ Gifts are always good to have on hand even if you end up handing them out before Christmas. Sometimes a friend just needs cheering up, and a surprise gift in the post is a real boost.

◆ At the festive time of year, buy and wrap a few generic 'male' and 'female' gifts, and keep them in your car or handbag in case someone surprises you with a present.

◆ If you really dislike some of your gifts, it's OK to exchange them – just don't ram your dislike for them down the giver's throat. Quietly sit down with your presents and gather up the ones you want to exchange, then make one assault on your high street and the various exchange queues. Do it sooner rather than later (yes, tear yourself away from *Sex and the City* repeats and Ferrero Rocher) because all the prices will be dropping in the January sales.

◆ When you're packing for a holiday, write a list of everything you need, and tick it off as it goes in. Wrap toiletries in plastic bags in case they leak.

◆ Pack a plastic bag and place all your dirty washing in it as the holiday evolves. This will keep your suitcase neat and help with laundry on your return.

◆ Organise your journey: pack adequate snacks and entertainment (cost-cutting airlines are trimming both of these things). Put drinks, nuts, fruit, magazines and an iPod into your carry-on luggage.

◆ Pre-book an aisle seat or emergency exit seat for extra legroom.

◆ Plan your travelling journey with care – don't wear restrictive clothing or high heels. You can wear a tracksuit and trainers and still look clean and smart.

◆ When you arrive in a foreign country, make sure you have even a little of the local currency for tips and taxis. Take a minute to work out what is what.

◆ Pack for different situations. Even if you're going skiing, pack a swimsuit in case there's a hot tub. Take long trousers in case you need to cover your knees to enter a local temple.

◆ Don't go mad with strange holiday buys. You know they'll be hidden at the back of the closet on your return. When you're weighing up buying something, think realistically about whether it has a use and whether or not it would fit in with your home decor.

◆ Edit and organise your holiday photos before you unleash them on your adoring public.

Index